THEORIES OF POPULATION
FROM RALEIGH TO ARTHUR YOUNG

THEORIES OF POPULATION FROM RALEIGH TO ARTHUR YOUNG

Lectures delivered in the
Galtonian Laboratory, University of London, under the
Newmarch Foundation, February 11 to March 18, 1929,
with two additional lectures and with references to
authorities

JAMES BONAR

Routledge
Taylor & Francis Group

LONDON AND NEW YORK

First published 1931 by Frank Cass & Co. Ltd.

New Impression 1966

This edition published 2013 by Routledge
2 Park Square, Milton Park, Abingdon, Oxfordshire OX14 4RN
711 Third Avenue, New York, NY 10017, USA

First issued in paperback 2016

Routledge is an imprint of the Taylor & Francis Group, an informa business

ISBN 13: 978-1-138-99822-3 (pbk)
ISBN 13: 978-0-7146-1274-4 (hbk)

CONTENTS

I

RALEIGH

(1552–1618)

THE STATISTICAL INSTRUMENT

THE EXAMPLE OF NEWMARCH

MUTUAL RELATIONS OF STATISTICS, ECONOMICS, DEMOGRAPHY

BOTERO ON POPULATION

ENGLISH HINTS IN SEVENTEENTH CENTURY

RALEIGH ON THE INDIVIDUAL AND THE SPECIES

BACON ON ENCLOSURES, PLANTATIONS, AND THE NEW WORLD

HOBBES, HIS "BELLUM", HIS CITIZEN, HIS LEVIATHAN

ELEMENTS IN PROBLEM OF POPULATION

In the study of human society the statistical instrument is one of those which we prove pragmatically, or by practice, without being able to define it to our entire satisfaction. John Mill, in the Introduction to his *Logic*, suggests that the definition of a science comes better at the end than at the beginning of the inquiries. We begin by using methods on trial; by and by, when they have stood the trial and helped us to get the knowledge we wanted, we may be able to state the limits of them and of the science they help. Professor Bowley, in his *Elements of Statistics* (chap. I), gives several definitions of Statistics, finding all of them instructive and no one of them complete. They are rather descriptions than definitions.[1]

If we take the most familiar—reasoning from the observed peculiar properties of large numbers—we may find the old derivation of "Stat-istics" from State roughly accurate, for at first it was only the State that collected large numbers, no one else having any use for them. Very much in the same way Economics would at first be Political Economy, every ordinary man being supposed to know all about Domestic by the light of nature and daily experience, and only the State (πόλις) caring to deal with the whole collectively. There was no thought in either case of going beyond man.

It is hardly necessary here to remark that Statistical inquiry, at first confined to human society, is in our time extended to any and every large group, and multitudes above and below man —for example, to what my friend Edgeworth called "unprogressive communities", bees and ants. 'Tis for one end, the good of man. We are going on the principle of Polonius: "By indirections find directions out", for man is meant to be benefited by our inquiries in the long run. In his *Mathematical Statistics*, lately edited by Professor Bowley, 1928, Edgeworth speaks of "mathematical reasoning applicable to physical phenomena quite as complex as human life" (p. 118). In common usage, of men that are careful enough not to identify statistics with mere numbers, statistics are numbers used with a purpose, figures ranged together with an end in view, if possible for some general conclusion, helping man whether evidently or not evidently; and, as large numbers are the best basis for the general conclusions, a study is eminently statistical that deals with such, and takes advantage of the known property of large numbers, warranting a probable result where small numbers warrant no general inference at all. As long as you are sure you are dealing with like units, the same kind of things, then "numbers are strength". How large must the numbers be in order to generate a general rule? We may not be able to define this lower limit exactly; we must often allow it to vary as our opportunities vary for getting hold of as many instances as we should like. Possibly our accomplished friends who deal with cosmic figures of population are as much embarrassed sometimes by their large figures as we are by our small ones. These questions are not on our programme; and, as to the competing senses of the word Probability,[2] here at least, being on the common highway of Statistical inquiry itself, we may surely venture to use Probability in the sense of *statistical frequency*.

I dare not enter farther on questions of principle in this temple of accurate statistics. Statistics are a Two-headed Janus, with one face turned to the Higher Mathematics, the other to the humbler Economics.[3] We are not renouncing the one because we follow the other. Though back to back, they are, for presentation of the complete result, inseparable. We were reminded the other day[4] that the great Faraday preferred to state his physical investigations in non-mathematical language, leaving Clerk Maxwell to make sure that they were in strict harmony with mathematical calculation. In our own modest range of study, *William Newmarch*,[5] to whose name and fame these lectures are due, enables me to plead his example when I take up a statistical subject on its less severe side. He was perhaps best known to the world as the continuer of Thomas Tooke's *History of Prices and of the State of the Circulation during the years* 1793 *to* 1856, in 6 vols., published 1838 to 1857. Newmarch contributed to the last two volumes substantially all except the passages dealing with Corn. This meant that he dealt with "the general course of trade, the progress of railway construction, the history of free trade from 1820 to 1856, the commercial and financial policy of France, the new supplies of gold from California and Australia", says Professor Hewins, in the *Dictionary of National Biography*. These are large and important studies, but the subjects are treated on what I have called the less severe side. The studies are statistical, but not obtrusively mathematical.

My programme is a modest one, but I trust it is in the spirit of the work of Newmarch. I desire simply to select one or two conspicuous instances where men of outstanding ability groped their way to the light on the field of Demography during the seventeenth and eighteenth centuries. We begin from the period when neither Statistics nor Economics nor Demography was clearly conceived, especially in England; and we pass into the period where statistical methods and economic principles have been more or less firmly grasped and used in alliance with each other.

It is true that the name *Demography* (description of the people) was first used by the Frenchman Achille Guillard[6] in 1855, the other two names, Statistics and Political Economy, being current some time before and more familiar even now. But Demography is a happy term for what Levasseur describes as the scope of it: "A study of human life in births, marriages and deaths, a study of the relations thus arising and the general state of the population occasioned thereby." The term "demographical" is perhaps the most convenient to use of, and in, this course of lectures, if Levasseur's description is kept in mind, including both the collection of the figures and the attempts to arrive at general principles.

In England, say in the year 1600, we had not arrived at general principles. In Italy they had been formulated by Giovanni Botero,[7] a Piedmont official, and more successfully by him than by the great Machiavelli, who left only a few shrewd hints of a contrary character to Botero's. Botero wrote in 1589 a book on the "Rationale of Government", if we may so translate *Ragione di Stato*, adding to it a *Treatise on the Greatness and Magnificence of Cities*. It is this last that contains the theory of population: "The growth of cities proceeds partly from the generative powers of men, partly from the nutritive powers of the cities. The powers of generation are the same now as one thousand years ago, and, if they had no impediment, the propagation of men would grow without limit and the growth of cities would never stop. If this growth does not go on, it must be from want of nourishment and means of support. Now, the nourishment is drawn either from the country round or from abroad, and, if the city is to go on growing, food must be brought to it from a distance."[8] "Though at the height of Roman greatness men's generative powers were just what they were at the beginning of Rome, yet the people did not grow in proportion; the nutritive powers of the city could not go farther; so that in process of time the inhabitants, not having a greater supply of food, either did not marry, or, if they married, their children found themselves in less comfort or in actual want, and they went abroad for better luck. The Romans, to provide for this case, made choice of the poorest citizens and sent them to Colonies, where like transplanted trees they might better their condition and comfort, and so multiply." "For the same reason the human race, grown to a certain multitude, has not passed beyond it; and for three thousand years or more the world has been just as full of men as now, for the fruits of the earth and the supply of food do not allow a greater number of people."[9]

Botero's books were translated into French in his lifetime, but he fell out of notice in his own country. He was quoted by Anderson in his *History of Commerce* in 1787, and is mentioned by J. R. MacCulloch in his *Literature of Political Economy* in 1845. All we can say is that, like Cantillon and the Canadian John Rae, he was not quite forgotten, but not well remembered. He is not mentioned by Malthus; yet Malthus read Italian. Certainly he seems unknown to our writers in the seventeenth century. Italian economics did not make their way to us across the frontiers as readily as poetry, novels, and plays. What we get in our own writers about the year 1600 is much more immature and amateur than Botero. But they too speak of Cities and Colonies, and they too speak of the Romans.

We need to remember that they are putting their

own questions in their way, not our questions in our way. The answers to ours can sometimes be gathered incidentally from them (e.g. in Raleigh's case) if we read between the lines. At the same time we need to take care that they are not really putting old questions and repeating by rote old answers.

Their style of writing is not what we expect now from anyone dealing with a scientific subject. They are fond of filling folios and quartos. Many of them in the seventeenth century seem to have no medium between the very short aphorism, which is a conclusion without a reason, and the long oration, which may be equally dogmatic. Length is not logic, any more than brevity; it is quality and cogency that matter. They seem to us to spend too much time over the oldest theories and histories of population; for example, those of the Book of Genesis, where man is pictured as having the world all before him, the possibilities of the globe still undeveloped, the whole earth his America. In political philosophy we hear too much of Greek and Roman examples, Greek and Roman institutions; and the Israelites are frequently in the foreground.

Sir Walter Raleigh and Bacon may introduce the century for us. Raleigh passed twelve years in the Tower of London studying chemistry[10] and writing his *History of the World*. In his romantic career under Elizabeth he had founded Virginia, thereby making a eugenic contribution to the composition of what we now call the United States, then the American Colonies. His enormous folio has the two drawbacks above mentioned, too much of Moses and Livy, too many old answers to old questions. Against Bodin (1520–96) and Machiavelli, he would not advocate attempts to increase the population by encouragement of marriage on the model of Augustus. He wrote a *Discourse of War in General*, where he describes the General War, the natural or necessary war, as that which is caused by the "natural necessity" of a country "overlaid by the multitude which live upon it"; it is compelled to "lay the load upon others by right or wrong, for, to omit the danger of pestilence, often visiting them which live in throngs, there is no misery that urgeth men so violently unto desperate courses and contempt of death as the torments and threats of famine".[11] We might have expected some distinction between (*a*) the Plague that takes all and sundry and (*b*) the War that picks the physically best. War caused by the need of your neighbour's land is an idea as old as Plato (*Rep.*, II. 374). Still, Raleigh has the root of the matter in him and is not surprised like many of his neighbours to find that Spain, to say nothing of England, was not depopulated either by wars or colonies.

His light is not so clear as Botero's, and perhaps we get more from his hints than from his expositions.

Take the following two passages from the *History of the World*—one dealing with the individual, the other with the species. The one reads like a forecast of Leibnitz,[12] the other of Charles Darwin. In his Preface he tells us he has suffered from prejudices excited against himself, Raleigh indeed having plenty of rivals and enemies; he says it is not enough to know that you are right and your slanderers wrong: "It is not truth but opinion that can travel the world without a passport. For were it otherwise and were there not as many internal forms of the mind as there are external figures of men, there were then some possibility to persuade by the mouth of one advocate, even equity alone.[13] But such is the multiplying and extensive virtue of dead earth [? influence of diverse climes] and of that breathing life which God hath cast upon slime and dust, as that among those that *were* (of whom we read and hear), and among those that *are* (whom we see and converse with), every one has received a general picture of face and every one a divers picture of mind, every one a form apart, every one a fancy and cogitation differing, *there being nothing wherein nature so much triumpheth as in dissimilitude.* From whence it cometh that there is found so great diversity of opinions, so strong a contrariety of inclinations, so many natural and unnatural, wise, foolish, manly and childish affections and passions in mortal men. For it is not the visible fashion and shape of plants and of reasonable creatures that makes the difference of working in the one, and of condition in the other, but the form internal." Notwithstanding (he adds), let men dissemble as they choose, sooner or later the character will appear in the face.

A few writers, like Buckle, whose *History of Civilization* appeared seventy years ago (1858), may have glorified Statistics (as his critics said he did) at the expense of the individual;[14] but no statistician who looked at the gallery of portraits in this building,* those "silent faces of the great and wise", could believe in the conflict of the two. That there is a truth in large numbers which does not come to light in the individual does not mean that there is no source of light and leading in the individual, and that we are trying to eradicate what Raleigh calls "dissimilitude".

There is a second quotation from Raleigh's *History* which affords a curious commentary on this very triumph of dissimilitude. In chap. VII of his First Book (§ 90, pp. 94–5), going on with his account of the "plantation of the world", he is discussing whether Noah's Ark was "of sufficient capacity" to hold all species, being a ship 600 feet long, 100 broad, and 60 deep (to give a free rendering of the original). He says that Noah did not need to take all we have now, but *all from which the present species are descended*; surely a very modern idea. Here are his words: "It is manifest and undoubtedly true that many of the species which now seem differing and of several kinds were not then *in rerum naturâ*. For those beasts which are of mixt nature,—either they were not in that age,

* Galtonian Laboratory.

or else it was not needful to preserve them, seeing they might be generated again by others, as the mules, the hyaena, and the like, the one begotten by asses and mares, and the other by foxes and wolves. And, whereas by discovering of strange lands wherein there are found diverse beasts and birds differing in colour or stature from those of these Northern parts, it may be supposed by a superficial consideration that all those which wear red and pied skins or feathers are differing from those that are less painted and wear plain russet or black, they are much mistaken that so think. And for my own opinion I find no difference but only in magnitude between the cat of Europe and the ounce of India, and even those dogs which are become wild in Hispaniola, with which the Spaniards used to devour the naked Indians, are now changed to wolves and begin to destroy the breed of their cattle and do also oftentimes tear asunder their own children. The common crow and rook of India is full of red feathers in the drowned and low islands of Caribana, and the blackbird and thrush hath his feathers mixed with black and carnation in the northern parts of Virginia. The dogfish of England is the shark of the Southern ocean, for, if colour or magnitude made a difference of species, then were the negroes, which we call the black mores [sic], *non animalia rationalia*, not men, but some kind of strange beast; and so the giants of South America should be of another kind than the people of this part of the world. We also see it daily that the natures of fruits are changed by transplantation, some to better, some to worse, especially with the change of climate. Crabs may be made good fruit by often grafting, and the best melons will change in a year or two to common Cowcummers by being set in a barren soil. Therefore, taking the kinds precisely of all creatures as they were by God created, or out of the earth by His ordinance produced, the ark by the measure of the common cubit was sufficiently capacious to contain of all" (p. 95). If this is not to be hailed as "Sir Walter Rawley his Truth", it is at least an advance on the idea of a straightforward increase and multiplication without other change than in the total numbers increased and multiplied.

Raleigh was dealing, like Edgeworth, with unprogressive communities, without Edgeworth's advantages from modern studies, and without any notion of applying the results to the one progressive community known to us. It is a bow drawn at a venture.

And perhaps his contemporary, Bacon,[15] was also saying better than he knew when he wrote in the essay "Of the Vicissitude of Things", in regard to the floods of people our forefathers were always seeing in their mind's eye pouring down on us from the North: "Look when the world hath fewest barbarous people but such as commonly will not marry or generate except they know means to live, *as is almost everywhere at this day except Tartary*, there is no danger of inundations of people."[16]

This very essay contains the famous passage, so characteristic of those times, so paradoxical, if not meaningless, in ours: "In the youth of a state, arms do flourish; in the middle age of a state, learning; and then both together. In the declining age of a state, mechanical arts and merchandise." In the essay on "Seditions and Troubles" he advises against multiplying the nobility and the clergy and scholars; it is the yeomen that are the best to fight our battles, and we must preserve them and set aside land for them,—as he observed was done under Henry VII. Otherwise enclosures cause a dangerous dearth of people. "Better a greater number that live lower and gather more." In the essay on "The True Greatness of Kingdoms and Estates" he says we do not want "great population and little strength". We should always be in a condition to fight; and in fact foreign wars do us good; they are not a curse but a blessing (ibidem).

He was not a political reformer; he seems to rest content with monarchy, and even a military monarchy. He made much of Naval power.

But his ideals lay elsewhere than in politics. His "New Atlantis" was not a social Utopia like Sir Thomas More's (1518). "This fable [says his editor] my lord devised to the end that he might exhibit therein a model or description of a college instituted for the interpreting of nature and the producing of great and marvellous works for the benefit of man under the name of Solomon's House or the College of the Six Days' Work. He thought also

in this present fable to have composed a frame of
laws or of the best state or mould of a commonwealth; but foreseeing it would be a long work his
desire of collecting the natural history diverted him
which he preferred many degrees before it." So
he left the New Atlantis at his death in 1626
incomplete, but probably much better so. Some of
its dreams have proved wonderfully true visions.
The best are not those of sensational inventions
like the aeroplane; "we imitate also the flight of
birds", but such as the idea of something like
a model Royal Society and College of Science,
nothing if not experimental. He sketches something
like a Board of Health, with Jewish coadjutors
versed in the shrewd ordinances of Leviticus. But
here is a scene in which modern biologists will
feel at home: "We have also parks and inclosures
of all sorts of beasts and birds, which we use not
for view or rareness, but likewise for dissections and
trials, that thereby we may take light what may
be wrought upon the body of man, wherein we
find many strange effects, as continuing life in
them, though divers parts which you account vital
be perished and taken forth." "By art likewise we
make them greater or taller than their kind is[17]
and contrariwise dwarf them and stay their growth;
we make them more fruitful and bearing than their
kind is, and contrariwise barren and not generative." We even, he says, produce new kinds by
"commixtures", and not barren, as people think
they must be.

This is a deliberate artificial variation of species; Raleigh was content to leave it to nature. There is, however, no word of statistics or demography. I do not think Bacon would have approached these even if he had made his ideal State, or even if, like Campanella (1568–1639), in his *City of the Sun*, he had revived the Platonic control of the breeding of his guardians.

He preferred for the State military strength above everything, power rather than plenty, security rather than opulence. If we blame him, we must remember Adam Smith's defence of the Navigation Acts ("Security is more important than opulence") in the year 1776. In the seventeenth century the English State was something much more fragile than in the eighteenth century, and needed every defence it could compass.

It did not need profound wisdom to say that the governing power should be as strong as possible. But, when we find in Bacon an essay on Plantations (XXXII), we wake up, for Plantations meant, or at least included, Colonies, and something more than mere Power would be necessary to judicious "planting".

In those days, however, the days of Raleigh and Bacon, the possibilities of the New World for anything but mines of gold and silver were little realized. Edmund Burke, in his famous speech of 1775 (March 22nd), spoke of the change as happening in the first half of his century. Before that, America "served for little more than to amuse you with stories of savage men and uncouth manners". Now, he said, "Whatever England has been growing to by a progressive increase of improvement, brought in by varieties of people, by a succession of civilizing conquests and civilizing settlements in a series of seventeen hundred years, you shall see as much added to her by America in the course of a single life." A hundred and fifty years after Burke, in our own time, the admirers of America might be tempted to give a new turn to an equally famous passage of Bacon himself, and say that in our time adversity is the lesson of the Old World and prosperity that of the New.[18] Bacon did not foresee these things; and at best we expect to hear his views on the services rendered by the "Plantations" to the people at large in view of examples in his own day. He does, indeed, regard them; he tells us what sort of men should be sent out and what supplies prepared for them, and what kind of land should be selected. He advises that the natives should occasionally be brought over here "that they may see a better condition than their own and commend it when they return". This exhortation to raise the native's standard of living shows that he did not agree with the praise of the Noble Savage as an object of imitation, in the manner of Dryden a century later, any more than he would have agreed with Isaac Watts and send us for models of conduct to the lower animals. He would at first send out men only; when the plantation "grows to strength, then", and apparently not till then, "it is time to plant with women as well as with men, that the plantation may spread into generations and not be ever pieced from without". As a matter of fact, the American Colonies grew in both ways. We should now all agree with him that there should be no piecing out with *convicts*, "a shameful and unblessed thing".

What reads to us most strangely is perhaps the first few sentences: "Plantations are amongst ancient primitive and heroical works. When the world was young, it begat more children, but now it is old it begets fewer, for I may justly account new plantations to be the children of former kingdoms." He is probably thinking not only of Celtic, Gothic, and Tartar invasions, but of the Roman custom of plantation of colonies, whereby, as he says himself, "the Roman plant was removed into the soil of other nations, and, putting both constitutions together, you will say that it was not the Romans that spread upon the world, but it was the world that spread upon the Romans; and that was the sure way of greatness", adopted, he thought, by Spain in his own day.

Bacon carries us away with his refreshing Tacitean brevity and impression of a wisdom that has always more behind than it has said. But science does not make progress *per saltum* by aphorisms. Among the sciences he directly stimulated demography was not one; and the crop of social and especially political Utopias arising in the generation after him was not of his raising, but was due to the religious and political uprisings of the "Puritan Revolution". We wonder why our questions were not put—e.g. how it is that, with certain reservations, the more men are afflicted the more they multiply and grow—and why, as Raleigh said, the old Spain was not depopulated by her colonies and wars, but has as many men as before. Botero, in Italy, had formulated the answer; but no one marked it. Macaulay, in a very rhetorical passage of his essay on Bacon in the *Edinburgh Review*, attributes to Bacon the lengthening of life and the advancement of all that ministers to the comforts and support of human beings. But, if political liberty is to count, he did not help us; and we must credit him simply with giving an immense stimulus to the scientific impulse, completing the revolt against the bondage of science in the Middle Ages, and foreseeing a Land of Promise that he never himself entered. Cowley was quite right; Bacon was the Moses who saw the land but did not enter it.

Hendriks[19] says truly of the Ancients that their study of vital statistics was confined to the causes of longevity, and Bacon seems never to have passed beyond this point of view. Witness his two essays on Death, where he moralizes finely and tells stories aptly without leading us scientifically a step farther than the gravedigger and Hamlet, who, according to a modern theory, may actually have been his creation.

One of the few passages in the *New Atlantis* that seem to us frivolous describes a way of fostering longevity by shutting up the old men like hermits in a cave.

But it is hard to quarrel with a man who drops such a saying as this from the same book: "The reverence of a man's self is, next religion, the chiefest bridle of all vices." Bacon has enough glory of his own without annexations from Stratford-on-Avon.

Harrington, who really goes beyond the ancients and teaches us a little demography, had absorbed both Francis Bacon and Thomas Hobbes. Hobbes, a somewhat less fine instrument, must be our next study before we pass to Harrington. Hobbes has an attractiveness of his own; he has very strong convictions. If he hits very hard he strikes at opposing views rather than persons, and his paradoxes trouble the waters of "use and wont", as did Mandeville's in the next century, to very good purpose.

Hobbes[20] is one of the greatest of our cynical philosophers, those who look by preference on the dark side of things and are constantly reminding us of our mortality and our selfishness. Such in the early eighteenth century were Swift and Mandeville, and in the nineteenth Carlyle and Ruskin. Their cynicism did not affect their vitality; they (all but one) reached threescore years and ten. Hobbes reached fourscore and ten, and he may have saved his strength by a convenient habit he had of reading few books but his own. He translated Homer in 1675, when he had passed eighty; and he wrote his *Behemoth*, a history in dialogue of the late Civil War, just before his death, which happened in 1679, in his ninety-first year.

He was the son of a clergyman, and had a good classical education; he went to Oxford and became tutor to a noble lord. We are sometimes told that even a great man (and of course every little one) is to be explained by his surroundings. By this convenient theory biographers of Bacon have explained away, not only his moral lapses in public life, but his intellectual defect of neglecting subjects which from the logic of his own principles would seem to have required his attention. But perhaps the environment of a great man explains rather the direction of his work than the greatness of it. According to Hobbes himself this is exactly true in his own case. Early in life he had planned out a system of philosophy in which he proposed to take the subjects in the following order: First Physics, then Human Physiology and what we now call psychology, and, after thus beginning with *things*, go on to *Man*, and his Civil Government, and what we now call Political Philosophy. Under the first head (of Physics) he thought Geometry had given an excellent foundation for the later Study of Man; if (said he) we only knew man as well as by geometry's help we know the heavens and the earth, then we should know the road to human happiness.[21] "Were the nature of human actions as distinctly known as the nature of quantity in geometrical figures, the strength of avarice and ambition which is sustained by the erroneous opinions of the vulgar, as touching the nature of right and wrong, would presently faint and languish, and mankind should enjoy such an immortal peace that unless it were for habitation, on the supposition that the earth should grow too narrow for her inhabitants, there would hardly be left any pretence for war." The original (*ut non videatur, nisi de loco, crescente scilicet hominum multitudine, unquam pugnandum esse*) seems better rendered "*unless for the sake of room*, the population growing, there would be no need for war".[22]

His hand was forced by the events of the times; Civil Government, intended to be the last of his studies, became the first—*De Cive* (*On the Citizen*) appearing in 1646 (date of preface), when the author was abroad. The other studies are not well remembered. Milton, whose hand was forced in the same way, had a very unlike experience; his political works are not what we most value; in Hobbes we value nothing so much as the *De Cive* and the *Leviathan* (1651).

England was divided against itself for twenty years (say, 1640 to 1660). To Hobbes the state of nature was War of all against all, but it seemed to him that, with the State once formed, war should be impossible. In making the State and in making man a Citizen thereof the people had made a compact with their ruler to save them from war; in the supreme interest of Peace they must obey him; and in England flagrantly they had not done so in those twenty years.

It was certainly in this case not the confined room that caused the fighting; it was disputes about religion, passing into disputes about political liberty. Hobbes in effect sets it all down to defective education; the nation did not understand the nature of a commonwealth. True, they were spared the worst excesses of his natural "war of all against all"; in the Civil War men were combatants (in Platonic phrase) who knew they were one day to be reconciled. In the extreme case the struggle is endless, for men are (roughly speaking) equal to each other not only in physical powers, but in intellect: hardly a modern doctrine.

The notion of this war of all against all has exerted an influence beyond its merits. It might seem to have an affinity with our modern notion of the struggle for existence, of all living creatures for room and food, each having the will or the instinct to live. The struggle, however, is different in quality when translated into terms of humanity. Even savages are not simply animals; they look before and after if only a very little, and their will is not mere instinct. Hobbes may seem to have reduced Man in his state of nature to a mere animal, just as Malthus, speaking of the struggle, speaks at first too unreservedly of the "great restrictive law", with too little allowance for the distinction of civilized and non-civilized. Hobbes (in *Leviathan*, 83) escapes the charge. The bees and ants, which have little States of their own and make a sort of oasis in the desert of savagery, are really, he says,

33

quite unlike men. They have no ambition, envy, or hatred; they do not cavil at their rulers; they have apparently no language; they confound injury and accident; their agreement is no deliberate compact, but is made by mere instinct. We cannot reason from beasts to men. If even the bees and ants are beneath our notice in political philosophy, much more the other creatures; among them there could not be war, only struggle. But, where there is humanity, in the state of nature, there is war; we may expect to find it if we go far enough back; and quite as necessarily, though artificially, there arises the compact which ends war and makes the commonwealth (*Leviathan*, chap. XVII, 84), none the worse for being artificial. "By art is created this great Leviathan or Commonwealth or State" (*Lev.*, Introd.).

Why does he choose the word? He writes: "Hitherto I have set forth the nature of a man whose pride and other passions have compelled him to submit himself to government, together with the great power of his governor, whom I compared to Leviathan, taking that comparison out of the two last verses of the one and fortieth of Job,[23] where God, having set forth the great power of 'Leviathan' [*balaena*, or whale], called him King of the proud"—"the king of all the children of pride". Hobbes had read also the fourth verse of that chapter of Job; "Canst thou draw out Leviathan with an hook? Will he make a covenant with thee? Wilt thou take him for a servant for ever?" With the human leviathan, unlike Job's, it is possible to make a firm contract.

Hobbes finely adds: "There be those that maintain that there are no grounds nor principles of reason to sustain those essential rights which make sovereignty absolute. For, if there were, they would have been found out in some place or other, whereas (say they) we see there has not hitherto been any commonwealth where those rights have been acknowledged or challenged[24] [claimed]. Wherein (says Hobbes) they argue as ill as if the savage people of America should deny there were any grounds or principles of reason so to build a house as to last as long as the materials, because they never yet saw any so well built. Time and industry produce every day new knowledge. And, as the art of well building is derived from principles of reason, observed by industrious men, that had long studied the nature of materials and the divers effects of figure and proportion, long after mankind began though poorly to build, so, long time after men have begun to constitute commonwealths imperfect and apt to lapse into disorder, there may principles of reason be found out, by industrious meditation, to make their constitution, excepting by external violence, everlasting. And such are those which I have in this discourse set forth."

Observe his confidence in the eternity of his system; it was a common failing of system-builders in his time, and is not entirely absent now. The "external violence" would seem to be caused by the pressure on space, struggle for room. "The multitude of poor and yet strong people still increasing, they are to be transplanted into countries not sufficiently inhabited, where nevertheless they are not to exterminate those they find there, but constrain them to inhabit closer together and not to range a great deal of ground to snatch what they find, but to court each little plot with art and labour to give them their sustenance in due season. And when the world is over-charged with inhabitants, then the last remedy of all is War, which provideth for every man by victory or death" (*Leviathan*, ch. XXX, p. 181, ed. 1651, p. 158, Morley).

If we ventured to generalize at all about the two centuries to which our study is confined, we might say that the problem of population was to the seventeenth century a problem of *room*, to the eighteenth of *food*; and *we* now take it (provisionally) as a problem of the *standard of living*, involving the other two essentials, but including the larger conditions of civilized life.

Such generalizing is not quite fair to the theorists. It suggests that they could only think of one element at a time. Occasional hints of the others are bound to occur, though the one important in their eyes may seem to us to cause neglect of the other two. Perhaps we should not generalize by centuries at all. The division into centuries is made by the historians for their convenience, and is not respected by the movements of thought any more than by the movements of armies or revolutions. We are taking the two centuries in these lectures because they are enough, and more than enough, for six lectures; but we try to follow the thought without fancying that it became different in 1601 or in 1701 from what it was in 1600 or 1700.

To divide the periods of it by monarchs would not be logically better, but it would give us more concrete associations to serve as the background of the text.

Let us say, then, that at the end of the Elizabethan period, "the spacious times of great Elizabeth", the times of great "Eliza and our James", there was no political economy, but there was a plenty of economic ideas and hints; there was no demography, but there were some demographic ideas and hints. The two could not be conjoined at that time in one statistical study, for they did not exist anywhere as "disciplines", if that means well-ordered studies distinguished from others, whether cognate or dissimilar. Contributions to them were often incidental to political theories, and drawn out by criticism of previous political theories. Hobbes never forgets Grotius,[25] who took a less cynical view of the Social Contract than his. We shall find in James Harrington a perpetual commentary on the political theories of Hobbes. But there is no going back. We get hints from Harrington succeeded afterwards by something better than hints even on demography.

REFERENCES TO CHAPTER I

1. Bowley, *Elements*, 2nd ed., 1902, pp. 3-18.
Rümelin, *Aufsätze*, 1863-74, pp. 208 seq.
2. Keynes, J. M., *A Treatise on Probability*, 1921, p. 96.
3. Dante's "Empire", looking to Rome, turning its back on Egypt. *Inferno*, XIV. 103.
4. In a *Times* leader of February 6, 1929.
5. Newmarch, born 1820, died 1882.
Professor Hewin's account of him is useful, and so is Dr. Lippert's in the *Handwörterbuch der Staatswissenschaften*, 1893, vol. V, p. 27. Dr. Lippert was librarian of the Statistical Bureau, Berlin. His list of works seems exhaustive. See also the obituary in the *Statistical Journal*, March 1882, pp. 115-121.
Thomas Tooke, born 1774, died 1858.
6. See René Gonnard, *Population* 1923, p. 334. Cf. *Statistical Journal*, March 1924, p. 301.
Statistik is the title of a book by Achenwall, 1752, though the adjective occurs in 1672. *Economie Politique*, Montchrétien, appeared in 1615. See also Roscher, *History of German Economics*, pp. 466 and 1011 of the original ed., 1874.
7. Botero, 1540-1617.
Machiavelli, 1469-1527.
8. Ad. Smith put the case tersely two hundred years afterwards: "Every man in a town must be fed by another in the country." *Lectures of* 1763, ed. Cannan, p. 230.
9. Botero, *Della Ragione di Stato*, etc., 1589, pp. 359-365, quoted by Professor Filippo Virgilii, *Il Problema della Popolazione*, Milan, 1924, pp. 42 seq. The passage is quoted at length by Adam Anderson, who may have been guided to it by Moreri's *Historical Dictionary*, 1643.
See Anderson's *History and Chronological Deduction of the Origin of Commerce ended* 1787, vol. II, p. 176 (the first was in 1764).
MacCulloch, *Literature*, 1845, p. 253.
10. With the Governor's lady abetting him, says Sir Allen Apsley's daughter, Mrs. Hutchinson, in her *Memoirs* of her heroic husband, Colonel Hutchinson (Bohn's ed., pp. 14, 182). Sir Allen himself was the Governor.
11. Quoted by Professor Stangeland, *Premalthusian Doctrines of Population*, New York, 1904, p. 112, from Works of Raleigh, 1751, vol. II, 25.
The Platonic passage is *Republic*, II. § 374.
For the two senses of *population* "action de peupler", "résultat

de cette action", see Schöne, *Population française*, 1893, p. 2, and compare our two uses of *publication*.

12. Leibnitz held the Identity of Indiscernibles; Things that are not *distinguishable* are not *different*.

13. It would be enough to be in the right.

14. See, e.g., Acton's *Historical Essays and Studies* (Macmillan), 1919, pp. 308–321 (article on Buckle, written 1858).

15. Francis Bacon, born in London 1561, died there 1626. The quotations are from the *Essays*, 1597, LVIII, p. 156, of Bell and Daldy's ed. 1866, and from the same, pp. 42, 91, Essay XV; p. 84, Essay XXIX; *Atlantis*, pp. 304, 300, cf. 297, 293; *Henry VII*, 361.

16. So Hobbes in *Behemoth* (18): "After the Inundation of Northern people had overflowed the Western parts of the Empire."

17. We saw something of the kind in this room not long ago in connection with colour in dogs, with Professor Karl Pearson as the magician. For the "room" see p. 21 note.

18. "Prosperity is the blessing of the Old Testament, adversity is the blessing of the New."—Essay V, of *Adversity*, p. 14. "Plantations," Essay XXXIII, 97, 95, 86.

19. *History of Insurance*, 31.

20. Thomas Hobbes of Malmesbury, 1588–1679. His printer, Crooke, says he had *Behemoth* from him in 1672 (Preface to ed. of 1682).

21. "Reason is reckoning", he writes in *Leviathan*, chap. V, p. 18 (1st ed., 1651).

22. Compare *De Cive*, 1647, I. § 13, § 15. The passage above discussed is from the *De Cive, Epistola Dedicatoria*, translated by Henry Morley in *Leviathan*, 1886. "Men equal in intellect", etc., *Leviathan*, XIII. 60, 61; Morley, 63–65.

23. Behemoth (either rhinoceros, hippopotamos, or crocodile, critics are not agreed which) occurs not far off, viz. Job xl. 15. In Milton, *Paradise Lost*, VII. 412, Leviathan is the whale; so here. "The nature of a man." Such is the reading of the first edition, 1651, and not "of man" as in Morley, 146. See 1st ed., chap. XXVIII, 166, 167. "Finely adds"—XXX. 176, Morley 154.

24. In the Latin translation, which is his own (1668), we have simply *agnita tamen*, with nothing corresponding to "challenged".

25. Grotius: 1583–1645. His book *De jure belli et pacis* appeared in 1625.

II

HARRINGTON

(1611–1677)

Harrington lived in stirring times. England was then passing through an era of excitement not unlike that of France in 1789. Milton's *Areopagitica* describes it for us in well-known terms. 1640 may be taken as the first date, the year when the Parliament wrested the reins of government from Charles I. We might have expected a ferment such as stirred France and all Europe in and after 1789, when Godwin and Condorcet dreamed dreams and saw visions. We demographers might have hoped to have had some modest gleanings, as we had from Malthus at the later epoch. We were not entirely unfortunate, but at first Church and State had chief place. The common feature of all such revolutions was exhibited in the tendency to describe the new era as the return to an older (*Redeunt Saturnia regna*), in this case to that of Magna Charta and the days when every peasant had his fowl in the pot. Men were excited by the idea of a New World, existing either sensibly in space or fancifully in their visions, a world in which we should all begin to be better men; and yet they liked to feel their foothold on the Old World, and, improving on the old adage "nothing new under the sun", they would say, "America is here or nowhere."[1] The Reformers of the Parliamentary era were not really content with going back to Magna Charta; and the standard of living was not falling but rising. Milton's political tracts (1641 seq.) took up the wondrous tale, and the writings of Hobbes

(1646 seq.) were to furnish criticism, though they stood up for the old ways in an offensively new way.

James Harrington, born at Upton, Northampton, in 1611, died 1677, was sent in 1622 to Trinity, Oxford, but left it without a degree[2] to travel on the Continent. According to Wood, under 632, § 95, he was "a handsome man of a delicate curled head of hair", shown by his portrait in *Political Discourses* 1660, and in Lely's *apud* Toland. He was of noble descent, and apparently well to do in the world. Living quietly and obscurely for some years, he was stirred up (he tells us) by the trumpet of Civil War[3] which broke the sleep of the nation under "Morpheus", James I. He had been brooding like the rest, to better purpose than most of them. For posterity he is the man of one book—Oceana, an ideal England. There is a story of a visit of his to Lady Claypole, daughter of the Protector, and of his playfully pretending to steal the Lady's little daughter, because, he said, "Your father has done the like with my child"—the MS. of his book. Cromwell had indeed laid hands on it, and, though assured by the author that it was only a harmless political romance, like *Utopia*, he was slow to give it back till Harrington's stroke of humour caused the daughter to intervene. The story is as much or little credible as that in Bacon's *Apophthegms* about the appeal to Elizabeth to release the Gospels from prison. It is Court gossip. But this is certain : that Cromwell became Protector in 1653, that Harrington tells his readers he began his book in 1654,[4] that it had three printers, that they finished their work in 1656, and that it appeared as a folio of 200 pages with the author's name, in that year, dutifully dedicated to his Highness the Lord Protector of the Commonwealth of England, Scotland, and Ireland.

Though Harrington (according to Toland[5]) was present at the execution of Charles, and might surely have been above suspicion, there was a good deal in the book that might have caused searchings of heart to the Protector. In later years, after Cromwell's death in 1658, and, when "suspect" at the Restoration of 1660, Harrington expressly declared that Cromwell was not his hero, he was never the man to introduce the Commonwealth of Oceana; he alone had the power to do it, but he wanted the will.

It was certainly not of Cromwell's kind; nor, I fear, could the most laboured special pleading procure favour for it with the restored King, Charles II. *Leviathan* would have been more to the King's mind. Yet Harrington pleads against a critic in these later days: "the model [we should say this ideal government] is not proposed to show the truth of fact, or that there has been such exactly in practice, but to show the truth of nature, or that such a model is practicable, wherefore he [the critic] need not to have alledged that it has not the truth of fact, which we all know, but to show where it fails of such truth in nature as can in any way render it impracticable."[6]

A model (he says) has three tests: "It must be wholly void of any contradiction or inequality; it must be such in which no number of men, having the *interest*, can have the power or strength,—and no number of men, having the power or strength, can have the *interest* to invade or disturb the government."

There is a ring of Godwin, of Robert Owen, of Bentham, in this. There is also a touch of Milton, Milton the politician. But Harrington is of his own time and his own type. The title of his third book, containing the *Art of Lawgiving*, and further explaining the *Oceana* generally, runs so: "A model of popular government, giving practical proposals according to reason, confirmed by the Scripture, and agreeable to the present balance or state of property in England" (Toland, 429). "They (these proposals) depend on principles of human prudence, being good without proof of scripture, but nevertheless such as are provable out of scripture." Aristotle's *Politics*, or the tenor of it, "Government depends on property", gives him his cue, and Bacon's *Henry VII* helps him by championing the yeomanry. But he handles the matter in his own way (*Prerogative apud* Toland infra, and *Oceana*, Introduction). With all his baldness of exposition, he has given us a book full of ideas, telling epigrams, and apt similes. More than one hundred years afterwards he was the favourite writer of John Adams,[8] a founder of the United States. Harrington writes, for example: "The errors of a people are occasioned by their governors." "A magistrate not receiving his power from the people takes it from them, and to take away their power is to take away their liberty." "If your liberty be not a root that grows, it will be a branch that withers." "The Reason of popular government must come nearest to right reason." Harrington's *Oceana*, Ocean Island, meant England. The book was issued to the English public with the Horatian motto *"Mutato nomine, de te fabula narratur"*. Under feigned names, afterwards interpreted in full by a "key", we have the places and institutions of his time, and even the persons, among whom is Clphaus Megaletor, the Protector himself. Harrington, like most such founders from Moses to Mussolini, believed that his Commonwealth of Oceana once founded would last for ever,[8] even as that of Venice, "incomparable Venice", with her "immortal commonwealth". Without sharing his confidence, we may glance at the political scheme as being the context of what is at present our main interest. Some indeed will go farther and say it is not merely the context, and contend that political liberty enters into the standard of living, in which case Harrington's scheme is nowhere alien to us. In progressive nations the masses cannot be viewed as a simple quantity, to be diminished or multiplied or kept stationary. There is always a question of quality and the standard of living. Harrington, commenting on Bacon, remarks that the French, too, might be said to have their yeomanry, and *their numbers* were greater than ours; but in war we proved superior, our *quality* was better.[9] Then, as to the standard of living, the Pilgrim Fathers went out to seek religious liberty; they found, besides that, political liberty and larger plenty. Political liberty lay close to religious; and, as to the larger plenty, though the Plantations had not been founded to secure this, but to serve the Mother Country and bring wealth to her,[10] they did not fail to bring the material benefit to the colonists also. So Bacon's progress of science must needs bring benefit to human life. Every medicine is an "innovation". Bacon plants his New Atlantis beyond seas to avoid prejudice, "beyond both the Old World and the New". He, too, had meant to write a Model Commonwealth, his editors say. He at least devised a model scientific workshop, more profitable, perhaps, than the other model would have been.

Harrington's editor, Toland, compares him to Harvey. Harvey had discovered the manner of the circulation of the blood; Harrington the root of all political evil and the cure thereof. Medicine still holds by Harvey; we are not yet at one as regards Harrington, but in his main positions he still has followers.[11]

His first main position is "Such as is the balance of dominion in a nation, such is the nature of her empire" (p. 86). In our words, government depends on property, especially property in land; and the only free strong permanent commonwealth is that in which there is a limit fixed to the value of the land that may be held by private persons. Harrington would fix this *upper* limit at £2,000 a year—which happens to be the figure of our supertax (1928) at its *lower* limit, and £2,000 meant very much more in 1656 than in 1928.

It does not seem a very irksome limit; but Harrington is no "Leveller" or Communist;[12] he would not even have *novae tabulae*, a general remission of debts, the old "slogan" of a Revolutionist; he thinks his own plan better than an equal division, which (he says) amongst other drawbacks leaves no employers.

£2,000 is the limit for England; but in Scotland only £500. Scotland is a poorer country, and the great drawback there is the nobility; "the people are little better than the cattle[13] of the nobility." "In the matter of your auxiliaries", he says, addressing the Englishmen who remembered the help rendered by the Scottish army a few years before, "Scotland will be of greater revenue to you than if you had the Indies. For whereas heretofore she has brought you forth nothing but her native thistle, ploughing out the rankness of her aristocracy by your Agrarian [law], you will find her an inexhaustible magazine of men, and to her advantage."

Ireland is to be colonized with Jews, who are to be invited to make it their Land of Promise, and are to have full use of all their customs, and full possession of their land farmed out to them and their heirs for ever, under the English Agrarian (of £2,000) and as a province of England. They prospered as agriculturists under the first Agrarian in Canaan, and will prosper again for their good and ours in Ireland under the new Agrarian. It may be remarked that after centuries of exclusion the Jews had just been readmitted into England by Cromwell. Bacon's recognition of them in the *New Atlantis* was the more daring as they were still excluded in his day.

Such, then, is the first of Harrington's proposals, the Agrarian law, which he says "will prevent any man or men from overpowering the whole people by possession of lands".[14] "Empire", or, as we should say, political power, comes from "goods of fortune", and the Agrarian secures that these shall not be wrongly "balanced". "Men are hung upon riches of necessity and by the teeth, forasmuch as he who wants bread is his servant that will feed him, and if a man thus feed an whole people they are under his Empire." Property in land gives a certain root or foothold; otherwise it (property) is "on the wing". In Holland and Genoa, it is true, there are signs that the balance of treasure from Trade may take the place of land. But Harrington's England was not the England of to-day; and "property" in his pages, unless otherwise expressly defined, always means property in land.

He goes on: Supposing that this Agrarian law has been carried out, and has secured power to the people, what is to be the Government, for government there must always be? First note that the people are to be under the rule of law, not of men. There should be an elected Senate to deliberate, and an elected Commons to legislate. "Out of the mouths of babes and sucklings" we learn how and why. There is an instructive children's plan for equal division when there is a cake to be divided between two children; one child says to the other, "*You divide and I choose*", i.e. I choose as I like out of the two pieces you set before me.[15] The key to the whole mystery of government is there, says Harrington.

There presently shows itself, whether amongst children or men, the phenomenon of *leadership*. There is an *authority* that comes from goods of the *mind*, as distinguished from Empire that comes from goods of fortune. He might well have added: We do not hang on goods of the mind by the teeth.

Where there is a crowd of men, or even a small gathering, there are always *leaders of men*. Get hold of these; let them be your Senate and counsellors, not to make your laws, but to lay them before your people. The Senate divide the cake; we must have another body, another Council, to do the choosing. The Senate propose; the People dispose, or, as he says, resolve. "For the wisdom of the few may be the light of mankind, but the interest of the few is not the profit of mankind, nor of a commonwealth."

This points to the need of organization, without

which the people (it is his own metaphor) are a *football crowd*.[16] We need "orders" of men and officials. So the second essential of Harrington's system, after the Agrarian as the first, is the *Rotation* of offices, helped out at a pinch by the Lot. The officials are to be elected by Ballot. Lot and Ballot were both suggested by Venice, the nearest approach to Harrington's ideal, only injuring herself by her confining of the franchise to a few.

Richard Baxter, whose *Holy Commonwealth*, 1659, was written, as its title says, "at the invitation of James Harrington, Esq.", quite approved of the Ballot in all cases "where there is danger lest the greatness of any overawe the people from their liberties" (256). Yet Baxter was no democrat; he went in that direction too far for the orthodox, not far enough for Harrington. Baxter's book had the honour of being publicly burned at Oxford in 1683.[17]

By the *Rota*, or plan of rotation, the officials are to vacate office after a fixed period, say three years. Thus, as the years go on, an increasing number of citizens will gain experience of political responsibility.

The idea of the Rota took hold of men studying public affairs just before the Restoration of 1660. There was a Rota Club devoted to debates on the subject.[18] It included prominent men like William Petty; and it even tried to influence Government. Masson (*Life of Milton*, vol. V, 481, 1877) makes mention of it; and Pepys was aware of its existence.

The larger proposals of Harrington seem to have had no followers organized into a society.

Doctrines as democratic as his are put forward by Marchmont Needham in the same year as *Oçeana*, 1656. His book, *The Excellency of a Free State*, has no constructive power; and it is surprising to find it reprinted for democratic propaganda over a hundred years afterwards, 1767, when Wilkes was flaunting the cap of liberty. Masson thinks Needham may have been inspired by John Milton, whose prose works are full of democratic fervour. Needham gives us the long-forgotten original of one of Sir Walter Scott's best stories.[19]

We hardly need to explore origins in the case of Harrington. The air was alive with new constitutions, to say nothing of Fifth Monarchies and Pre-Millennials. The Scriptures and the Latin and Greek classics provided the bricks and mortar for these quaint buildings. Harrington's was really less quaint and more solid than the rest, but you will find him using those very materials. He could not do otherwise in those days, when everybody knew his Bible and most had read their Caesar's *Commentaries* and their *Ethics* of Aristotle. But his main idea goes easily into modern language—the dependence of power on property.

This dependence of political power on the distribution of property in land is so far from leading him to make too much of material goods that he makes rather too little; we miss the material details. He pursues with ardour the details of the political machine, and even enters into programmes of legislation, the Army, the Craft Guilds, the Church, and Education. He and Milton were before their time in pressing for a popular and compulsory education.[20]

If the whole problem of the government of England seems easier in the pages of Harrington than it could be now, we must remember that the population of the United Kingdom at that time is believed to have been about five millions. But there was no general census, and there were few partial surveys.

Now at last we have a bit of demography. Harrington's Commonwealth was to be what he calls *"a commonwealth for increase"*.[21] He shared in the common feeling of his time that, though no one knew exactly how many people there really were in England, it was better the numbers should grow than stand still. His electors were to be fathers of families; the father of ten children was to pay no taxes, those that remained bachelors after twenty-five were to pay double taxes. "Forasmuch as the Commonwealth demandeth as well the fruits of a man's body as of his mind, he that hath not been married shall not be capable of these magistracies until he be married." And it is one of his arguments for his Agrarian that it would stop "the wretched system of marrying for money".

He believed, like John Milton, that his England was God's England, as the Canadians call Canada God's own land. His countrymen (he thought) had superior grit, and it was a duty to spread the Empire and bring the gospel of liberty[22] to other nations. We did this by our Plantations and Provinces, in the way now known as "peaceful penetration". In the "Provinces" of our Commonwealth the balance is not the same as in our Commonwealth itself. If the richest there were to have power according to their riches, the provinces would be no longer provinces but independent. One country dominates another not by the balance of land, which is an internal affair, but because its army is stronger, or it may have natural advantages of situation as the Danes have, in the control of the Sound. "For the colonies in the Indies, they are as yet babes that cannot live without sucking the breasts of their mother cities, but such as I mistake if [he means: I doubt whether] when they come of age they do not *wean themselves*, which causeth me to wonder at Princes that delight to be exhausted that way."

Hobbes[23] had spoken decidedly to the same effect; among the infirmities of a commonwealth is "the insatiable appetite, or βουλιμία, of enlarging dominion with the incurable wounds thereby many times received from the enemy, and the 'wens' of ununited conquests, which are many times a burthen, and with less danger lost than kept". He may have been thinking of Calais and Dunkirk, which were hardly colonies. Harrington more minutely compares the economic relation of colonies and mother country to city and country.

In the *Prerogative*,[24] the most important of his answers to critics, he is eloquent in the praise of London and cities in general. He has given some thought to the action and interaction of town and country: "One of the blessings that God promised to Abraham was that his seed should be multiplied as the stars of heaven. That the commonwealth of Rome by multiplying her seed came to bound her territory with the Ocean and her fame with the stars of heaven; that such a populousness is that without which there can be no great commonwealth, both reason and good authors are clear; but whether it ought to begin in the country or in the city is a scruple I have not known them make. That of Israel began in the country, that of Rome in the city. Except there be obstruction or impediment by the law, as in Turkey where the country, and in England where the city, is forbid to increase; wherever there is a populous country, as, for example, France, it makes a populous city as Paris; and wherever there is a populous city, as Rome, after the ruin of Alba, and Amsterdam, after the ruin, as to trade, of Antwerp, it makes a populous territory, as was that of the rustic [rural] tribes [of Rome], and is that of Holland."

"But the ways how a populous city comes to make a populous country and how a populous country comes to make a populous city are contrary, the one happening through suckling as that of the city, and the other through weaning as that of the country."

"For proof of the former—the more mouths there be in a city the more meat of necessity must be vented [vended or sold] by the country, and so there will be more corn, more cattle, and better markets, which, breeding more labourers, more husbandmen, and richer farmers, bring the country so far from a commonwealth of cottagers that, where the blessings of God through the fruitfulness of late years with us rendered the husbandman unable to dispute precedence with the beggar's bush,[25] his trade, thus uninterrupted in that his markets are certain, goes on with increase of children, of servants, of corn, and of cattle, for there is no reason why the fields adjoining the Emporium [London], being but a hard soil, should annually produce two crops but the populousness of the city."

"Their country then, growing more populous and better stocked with cattle, which also increases manure for the land, must proportionably increase in fruitfulness. Hence it is that the Romans[26] also were good at such works. In Holland there is scarce a puddle undrained, nor a bank of sand cast up by the sea that is not covered with earth and made fruitful by the people, these being so strangely with the growth of Amsterdam increased, as comes perhaps to two parts in three; nor, the Agrarian taking place in Oceana, would it be longer disputed whether we might not destroy fishes to plant men. Thus a populous city makes a country milch,[27] or populous by sucking; and, whereas some may say that such a city may suck from foreign parts, it is true enough, and nowhere more apparent than in Amsterdam. But a city that has recourse to a foreign dug e'er she had first sucked that of her proper nurse, or territory, dry, you shall hardly find; or, finding that (as in some plantation not yet weaned), will hardly be able to make that objection hold, seeing it will not lie so much against the populousness of the place as the country.

"But a populous country makes a populous city by weaning, for, when the people increase so that the dug of earth can do no more, the overplus must seek some other way of livelihood; which is other arms [other nurses]; such were those of the Goths and Vandals, or merchandise and manufacture, for which ends, it being necessary that they lay their heads and their stock together, this makes populous cities. Thus Holland, being a small territory and sucked dry, has upon the matter weaned the whole people, and is thereby become, as it were, one city that sucks all the world."

Far from threatening the liberty of the rest, the city contributes more than the rest to the general defence.

This is rough-and-ready economic theory. Harrington's point of view is almost always that of the agriculturist. It is hard to fit his particular scheme of "nationalization of the land" into the conditions of modern England, where what he calls mechanical labour, labour other than agricultural, so much predominates over agricultural. He thinks

57

that a nobility living on their own revenues are necessary to a commonwealth. "For how else can you have a commonwealth that is not altogether mechanic, or what comparison is there of such commonwealths as are to come nearest to mechanic, for example Athens, Switzerland, Holland, unto Lacedaemon Rome and Venice plumed with their aristocracies? Your mechanics, till they have first feathered their nests, like the fowls of the air whose whole employment is to seek their food, are so busied in their private concernments that they have neither leisure to study the public nor are safely to be trusted with it (*quia egestas haud facile habetur sine damno*) because a man is not faithfully embarked in this kind of ship if he have no share in the freight. But if his share be such as gives him leisure by his private advantage to reflect upon that of the public, what other name is there for this sort of men, being *à leur aise*, but, as Machiavel you see calls them, nobility"[28]—with their ancient riches, services, and virtues, inseparable from such. Though riches, as Bacon says, are the baggage of virtue (the *impedimenta*), they cannot be left behind. The nobility of Oceana are "the best of all other", because "they, having no stamp [or privilege] whence to derive their price have it no otherwise than by their intrinsic value". He evidently thought that the leaders would be always recognized and allowed to lead.

Yet he allows that even in his time the revenue of industry in a nation is three- or fourfold greater than that of the mere rent, and, if the people obstructed industry they would obstruct their own livelihood, and if they make a war they obstruct it. So again, when he is dealing with apprenticeships, guilds, and professions, he says that after fifteen the occupation chosen "with the many must be into the mechanics, that is to say, into agriculture, or husbandry, into manufactures, or into merchandise". Agriculture is the bread of the nation; we are hung upon it by the teeth; it is a mighty nursery of strength, the best army, and the most assured knapsack. A commonwealth of husbandmen, "and such is ours", is the best of all. He would, therefore, do everything to encourage it. Racking of rents is bad, for example. But the opposite, too easy renting, "too much ease given in that kind", causes sloth and destroys industry, the nerve of a commonwealth.[29] "In manufactured merchandise the Hollander hath gotten the start of us; but at the long run it will be found that a people working upon a foreign commodity doth but *farm* the manufacture, and that it is *entailed* upon them only where the growth of it is native; as also that it is one thing to have the carriage of other men's goods and another for a man to bring his own unto the best market. Wherefore Nature having provided encouragement for those arts in this nation above others, where, the people growing, they of necessity must also increase, it cannot but establish them upon a very more sure and effectual foundation than that of the Hollanders. But their

59

educations are in order unto the first things or necessities of nature, as husbandry unto the food, manufacture unto their clothing, and merchandise unto the purse of the commonwealth."

Harrington is not an oracle in political economy, whatever he is in political philosophy. We are all apt to be led astray by our metaphors; and Harrington was, I think, misled like so many others by the metaphor of the foundations. Agriculture is the foundation; therefore we should grow our own corn. As well say that because the foundations of a house are of transcendent importance we should lay them ourselves, instead of simply taking care that they are well laid, and then that the house is well built upon them after our own choice. He did not realize any more than the majority of his contemporaries that England was already entering of her own choice on the industrial policy pursued by Holland, who had no choice in the matter. Andrew Yarranton[30] not very long after him (1676, *England's Improvement by Land and Sea*) saw farther; and his editor, P. E. Dove, hails him as the greatest of modern discoverers because his idea was "To beat the Dutch without fighting", viz. by honest trade and industry. He foresaw the Bank of England and England's Iron Age. But he was, I fear, hardly the forerunner of the sage of 1776; his was to be no open trade, and he thought that wherever the country is full of people it is rich. He is much more concerned with the advancement of the several branches of English industry than with the establishment of any general principles of economics.

In mediaeval times the interest of the locality, and later even more the interest of the municipality and the Craft, were dominant. In Hales (if he be the "W. S." of a famous tract, 1581), and later in Mun, writing on *England's Treasure by Foreign Trade* (1664), there were signs of more regard for the interests of the nation as a whole and the idea of a balance of trade to secure the commonweal and *commonwealth*, i.e. that the various trading interests should be so balanced as to secure the greatest economic efficiency of the various elements, consistently with the prosperity of the *nation* as a whole. Mercantilism so called was really from this point of view an improvement on mediaevalism. It is true that its policy implied too great an attachment to the precious metals; there is a trace of this long after the power of "Mercantilism" had ceased. It is hardly true that mercantilism was always too much attached to mere populousness. Some mercantilists had this feature and some had not.

Unfortunately the notion that the Nation was to be chiefly considered became a narrowing influence, and we had England's national ambition to rule the waves converted into a cause of war against the Dutch. The great Selden said (1635) we must have a *Mare Clausum*; we must be supreme at sea as if we owned it. But against this narrowness we had the rise of a theory of natural rights and

61

international law, to which theory the Dutchman Grotius had converted no small part of the thinking world, statesmen or not.

It is possible that the idea of a balance of trade had its analogue in the idea of a balance of powers within the State and in its civil government. The word "balance" is there used especially by Harrington as a word to charm with. But the resemblance does not go very deep, and there is no sign that Harrington applied himself with any seriousness to what we should call economic theory.

Harrington's influence on demographic theory is of more special interest to us here. It may be called *indirect,* so far as his political models stirred up men who afterwards worked for demography, e.g. Petty; but so far as it came from his discussion of town and country, it is a *direct,* though not a large, influence. In his last years he had the usual experience of men who had been eminent under the Commonwealth. The Restoration Government of 1660 were afraid to trust him, though he had given many proofs that in the politics of his books he was far from irreconcilable. He was shut up in the Tower, December 1661, and in Portsea Castle for some years, and was released on medical grounds. He is said to have left the impression of weakening powers, and even of wandering in the mind.[31] But his English friends still believed in him; and they were quite able to tell enthusiasm from lunacy, visions from illusions.

His illusions are gone, but the essential part of

his visions is still with us. His own unessential part was laid by his friends, next Raleigh's, in St. Margaret's, Westminster, 1677.

NOTE TO CHAPTER II

DIARY OF SAMUEL PEPYS

January 10, 1659, N.S. 1660.—"To the Coffee House where were a great confluence of gentlemen: viz. Mr. Harrington, Poultny chairman, Gold, Dr. Petty etc., where admirable discourse till nine at night.

17th.—In our way to Kensington we understood how that my Lord Chesterfield had killed another gentleman about half an hour before and was fled. I went to the Coffee Club and heard very good discourse; it was in answer to Mr. Harrington's answer, who said that the state of the Roman government was not a settled government, and so it was no wonder that the balance of prosperity [read: property] was in one hand and the command in another, it being therefore always in a posture of war; but it was carried by ballot that it was a steady government, though it is true by the voices [votes] it had been carried before that it was an unsteady government; so to-morrow it is to be proved by the opponents that the balance lay in one hand and the government in another."

But "to-morrow" all his thoughts are—what Monk will do, and we hear no more of Harrington.

The title of a book printed in 1658 and ascribed to Dr. Laurence Womack may contain a reference to our author: *The Examination of Tilenus before the Triers in order to his intended settlement in the office of a Publick Preacher in the Commonwealth of Utopia.* For an amusing reference a hundred years afterwards see *The Trial of a Student at the College of Clutha [Glasgow] in the Kingdom of Oceana,* Glasgow, 1768, and the description of the incident in *R. and A. Foulis,* Glasgow, 1913, pp. 38, 39.

63

REFERENCES TO CHAPTER II

1. Wilhelm Meister, but Locke has it, *Civil Government*, II, XLIX. 201. "All the world was America."

2. Anthony Wood's *Athenae Oxon.* for 1500-1690, ed. 1691, p. 435.

3. Last paragraph of the Introduction to *Oceana*.

4. "Began his book in 1654." Epistle to the Reader, prefixed to *Oceana*, after the 1st ed., 1656.

5. John Toland's ed. of Harrington's *Works*, 1737, XVII—as to Cromwell, XXIX.

6. *Art of Lawgiving* (against Matthew Wren's *Monarchy Asserted*), reprinted in Toland, l.c. 462, cf. 429, 389, 395.
Aristotle, *Pol.* V. III. ix.

7. *Defence of the Constitutions of Government of the United States of America*, by John Adams, London printed and Boston reprinted, 1788, pp. 85, 100, 108. See *The Political Science of John Adams, a Study in the theory of mixed government and the bicameral system*, C. M. Walsh, Putnam, N.Y. and London, 1915.

8. "Lost for ever", *Oceana*, 1st ed., 84, cf. 54, Toland, 100. The previous citations are from *Oceana* 48, 127 (cf. 184), 261, of 1st ed. The key to names: Toland, p. xxi (*Life of Harrington*).

9. *Prerogative apud* Toland, 288, 289. If you want defence, you must grow men that can give it.

10. So even *Oceana*, 218, "Into the purse of the commonwealth".
Compare Bacon, *Essay on Innovations*, XXIV. 69.
Atlantis to be far away, *Atlantis*, 274, cf. 269.

11. The American John Adams was a follower. Acton's way of describing Lorenz Stein's adherence almost implies his own adherence. *Historical Essays*, 380, 391.

12. "No Leveller", *Oceana*, 113, 200, cf. 199.

13. Scotland, 87. Compare Introd., 2, and text p. 233 (1st ed.).
"Live stock", 112. There is no suspicion of "chattels" here. Harrington wrote in English, and he speaks of these cattle being "driven upon your grounds".
"Ireland", ib. 81 foot, compare 112 (Panoped).
"Jews", Introd., p. 2.

14. Security against aggrandizement of individuals, etc. *Oceana*, 22, 23, cf. 4, 5.
Trade, 5 foot.
Rule of law, 11.

15. P. 13, compare 158, 190, and 14. If you divide unequally, I can always choose the bigger of the pieces you put out for me.

16. P. 155. There was football on the earth in those days. Ballot, p. 28.

17. Wood's *Athenae Oxonienses*.

18. See Pepys, in Note, supra. 1659–60, January 10th and 17th, on Rome. Add September 2, 1667, on Matthew Wren.

We have something similar in our "Institute for the Study of International Affairs."

19. Masson, V. 433. The reprint was that of Richard Baron, whose *Free State* has Needham's deliverances in Part II, chap. V. Needham's Part II, chap. III, 64, contains the original of Scott's story in *Waverley* (the earthly crown and the heavenly). It had referred, not to Prince Charlie in 1745, but to Charles I a hundred years before him; and the preacher was an Irish bishop at the Hague: "They [the Presbyterians] deprived him of his earthly crown and kept him languishing, whereas [his own party say] others were more courteous in sending him to a heavenly one."

20. The Church and education, etc., *Oceana*, 205, 209.

Milton, *Free Commonwealth*, 1660.

21. Commonwealth for increase, *Oceana*, 22, double taxes 77, married men 79, cf. 108.

22. Gospel of liberty, ib. 258, 261, cf. 113. Provinces, 8, 9.

23. Hobbes, *Leviathan*, XXIX. 152, cf. XXIV end, where the distinction is put very neatly.

Cobbett called London "the Wen". See also Graunt, infra. $Bov\lambda\iota\mu\iota\alpha$ may be translated "beastly hunger".

24. Toland, 300, 301, cf. 389.

25. "Beggar's bush", etc. The meaning seems to be that the homeless beggar was as well off as he.

26. We do not escape from them and the Israelites till the end of the next century, and not entirely then.

27. "Mother of mine she [England] never was, but only foster-mother or milk cow", says Disraeli *apud* Carlyle: *Shooting Niagara. Miscell. Essays*, pop. ed., vol. VII, p. 208.

28. Nobility, etc., *Prerogative* 145, cf. 200, 217, 218.

Bacon, *Essay* "Of Riches", XXIV, p. 98.

29. Arthur Young was strongly of this opinion. See *Political Arithmetic*, 1774.

30. P. E. Dove, *Andrew Yarranton the Founder of English Political Economy*, Edin., 1854, p. 12, for his forecasts 31, 40, 52, limits 76, 45.

31. He told stories of an Italian journey that (Toland allows) he never took. It was said that he saw real "bees in his bonnet". See Wood's *Athenae Oxonienses*, 1st ed., 439. Toland, XXXVIII.

III

JOHN GRAUNT
(April 1620–April 1674)

WILLIAM PETTY
(1623–1687)

We cannot claim for Harrington a direct influence on demography. Others had written about great cities,[1] and the passage read contains only a hint, not followed up. But he seems to have influenced Petty, and Petty influenced John Graunt. Passing from Harrington to Petty we must break our journey at John Graunt, who, indeed, might well deserve a journey all to himself.

If Petty is an extraordinary man, Graunt is a very ordinary man; but he was an ordinary man who did an extraordinary deed. If Petty, as is sometimes said, founded Political Economy, it was John Graunt who founded Demography, the faithful statistical study of births, marriages, and deaths. His work on London became a model for work of the kind in any and every other city. Petty was the more learned and the cleverer man; but the demographical opportunities lay closer to the hand of Graunt, who had wit enough to seize them.

The political troubles of Charles I, the Civil War, and the Commonwealth were the fitting background for Harrington. The Plague, slaying its ten thousands and always coming back like the locusts in the Book of Joel, was a good historical setting for infant demography, drawing (as the Plague did) all men's attention to the growth of the Great City, and to its puzzling refusal to be permanently depopulated by the Plague or anything else.

Early in 1662 Graunt published a book on the

London Bills of Mortality, and sent fifty copies to the newly formed Royal Society, "the Royal Society of Philosophers meeting at Gresham College".[2] A committee (of the said Society), including William Petty, reported so favourably that Graunt was at once elected a member of the same. Graunt had previously, about 1646, helped Petty to the Chair of "Music", really Chair of Art in general, in Gresham College; and they were not strangers. At a later time, about 1667, Graunt helped Petty to import Walloon weavers into Ireland, and Petty begins his own *Observations on the Dublin Bills of Mortality*, 1681 (published 1683)[3] with a compliment to his predecessor: "*The Observations upon the London Bills of Mortality* have been a new light to the world, and the like observation upon those of Dublin may serve as snuffers to make the same candle burn clearer." Would he have written in this way if he had really meant what his title-page said, that the two were by one and the same "observator"? Petty seems divided between a desire to patronize Graunt and a longing to claim Graunt's achievement as his own.

The quaintest testimony to Graunt's reputation is Anthony Wood's inclusion of him among his Oxford Worthies, though Graunt had never been at either Oxford or Cambridge. Here is the entry, coming after an "Edward Grant" of forgotten fame: "Now I am got into the name of Graunt I cannot without the guilt of concealment but to let you know somethings [*sic*] of the most ingenious person, considering his education and employment, that his time hath produced. His name is John Graunt, born at the sign of the Seven Stars in Birchin-lane within the parish of St. Michael, Cornhill, in London, between 7 and 8 of the clock in the morn of the 24 of April 1620. Son of Henry Graunt a Hampshire man. Educated while a boy in English learning, bound an apprentice to a haberdasher of small wares, which trade he mostly followed, though free of the Drapers' Company. Afterwards he went through all the Offices of the City, as far as a Common Councilman, bearing that office two years. He was also Captain of the Trained-band several years, and Major of it two or three, and then laid down his trade and all public employments upon account of religion. For, though he was Puritanically bred and had several years taken sermon-notes by his most dextrous and incomparable faculty in short writing [we should say facility in shorthand writing] and afterwards did profess himself for some time a Socinian, yet in his latter days he turned Roman Catholic, in which persuasion he zealously lived for some time and died. He hath written (1) *Natural and Political Observations made upon the Bills of Mortality*, etc., London 1661, and 62 [really January 1662] in quarto afterwards in octavo with several additions; done upon certain hints and advice of Sir William Petty. (2) *Observations on the Advance of Excise*. And (3) something about Religion. But these two are not yet printed. He died on the

18 of April being Easter Even 1674, and was buried four days after in St. Dunstan's Church in Fleet Street, in the body thereof, under the pews towards the gallery on the North side, London. At which time his body was attended with a great number of ingenious persons; and among others, with tears, was that great vertuoso Sir William Pettie before mentioned. The said Joh. Graunt was an ingenious and studious person, generally beloved; was a faithful friend, a great peace-maker, and one that had often been chosen for his prudence and justice an arbitrator. But above all his excellent working head was much commended, and the rather for this reason that it was for the public good of learning which is very rare in a trader or mechanic."[4] After Ricardo and Grote, Goschen and Lubbock, we are less likely to be surprised to find wisdom coming from City Magnates.

The full title of Graunt's book is: "*Natural and Political Observations mentioned in a following Index and made upon the Bills of Mortality*. By John Graunt, citizen of London. With reference to the government, religion, trade, growth, air, diseases, and the several changes of the said City.

> Non me ut miretur turba laboro,
> Contentus paucis lectoribus."

The dedication, to Lord Roberts, is dated January 25, 1661, which to us means 1662. Petty's *Observations on the Dublin Bills of Mortality* did not appear till 1683. From the evidence carefully

71

digested by Professor Hull[5] it seems clear that
Petty who wept at Graunt's death was not the
writer of Graunt's book, but no doubt had helped
Graunt by his professional knowledge of medicine
and allowed Graunt to use any facts and figures
that were at Petty's better command. So we have
in Graunt details about a country parish, Romsey,
Hants, likely to be well known to Petty and not
to Graunt. Petty seems at one time to have counted
his contributions so considerable as to warrant a
claim to authorship; but he did not press the
claim, and we have no reason to doubt the sincerity
of his sorrow in 1674. Petty's powers had a much
wider range than Graunt's; and the public was
ready then as it is now to attribute a great
book to a man whose reputation is already great.[6]
Add that by and by, other things being equal,
the public would not praise a Roman Catholic.
These were the days of Popish Plots real and
imaginary.

Dr. Greenwood,[7] replying to the challenge of
Lord Lansdowne in the *Petty Papers*, makes out a
case from the internal evidence that seems to be
conclusively in favour of Graunt. No one could
speak with more authority, and I think most of us
will share his conclusion.

My friend and predecessor[8] in this place well
reminded us that the two men viewed the growth
of the City with very different eyes; to Graunt it
was a huge "pile", a head too big for the body;
Petty was proud to prove it bigger than Paris;

all arts and crafts are best economized when central-
ized: so he says in his *Growth of London*, 1682 (Hull,
469, and infra, page 86). It might be added that
Graunt speaks more respectfully of Agriculture than
Petty, "the fundamental trade which is husbandry
and plantation".[9]

There was some soul of goodness in the Plague.
It was the Plague itself that led to the Bills of
Mortality. Dr. Ogle[10] has traced one such Bill as
early as perhaps 1512. At first they waxed and
waned with the Plague, and were mainly a record
drawn up by the parish clerks, assisted by old
women searchers, of the burials in the City. Then
the baptisms were added. Graunt has noted the
changes in the forms of the returns between his
earliest, 1592, and the latest (of his first edition),
1662. Even his latest contain no record of marriages,
or of age at death. As a City magnate he had easy
access to documents. If he sometimes forgot to
return them, it was an incident not without parallel
in our own time.[11]

To the then indispensable Dedication made to
a great public man, Lord Roberts, he adds a second,
addressed to the President of the Royal Society,
Sir Robert Moray. To Roberts he writes that he
has reduced a confused mass to shape, added his
own *Observations*, and published the whole in a
pamphlet of two hours' reading, "hoping they
may be of as much use to persons in your lordship's
place[12] as they are of little or none to me, which is
of no more than the fairest diamonds are to the

73

journeyman jeweller that works them, or the poor labourer that first digged them from the earth. For with all humble submission to your lordship I conceive that it doth not ill become a peer of the parliament or member of his Majesty's Council to consider how few starve of the many that beg,—that the irreligious proposals of some to multiply people by polygamy are withal irrational and fruitless—that the troublesome seclusions in the plague time are not a remedy to be purchased at vast inconveniences—that the greatest plagues of the city are equally and quickly repaired from the country—that the wasting of males by wars and colonies do not prejudice the due proportion between them and females—that the opinions of plagues accompanying the entrance of Kings is [sic] false and seditious—that London, the metropolis of England, is perhaps a head too big for the body, and possibly too strong—that this head grows three times as fast as the body unto which it belongs, that is, it doubles its people in a third part of the time—that our parishes are now grown madly disproportionable—that our temples are not suitable to our religion—that the trade and very City of London removes westward,—that the walled city is but a fifth of the whole pile—that the old streets are unfit for the present frequency of coaches—that the passage of Ludgate is a throat too strait for the body—that the fighting men about London are able to make three as great armies as can be of use in this island[13]—that the number of heads is such as hath certainly much deceived some of our senators in their appointments of Poll money, etc. Now, although your lordship's most excellent discourses have well informed me that your lordship is no stranger to these positions, yet because I knew not that your lordship had ever deduced them from the Bills of Mortality, I hoped it might not be ungrateful to your lordship to see unto how much profit that one talent might be improved, besides the many curiosities concerning the waxing and waning of diseases, the relation between healthful and fruitful seasons, the difference between the city and the country air, etc. All which being new, to the best of my knowledge and the whole pamphlet not two hours' reading, I did make bold to trouble your lordship with a perusal of it."

Graunt writes with the confidence of knowledge and keeps his promises. He confronts vague scares with figures.[14] London had been spoken of as an overgrown monster that devoured its own offspring and was wasting away. To take the subjects in his own order as given in the above letter—London's starving beggars did not die in multitudes. The Weekly Bills of Mortality extant at the Parish Clerks' Hall from 1603 to 1660 show that of the 229,250 which died no more than 51 were starved, and most of the beggars now swarming in the City might quite well be kept under public control. He would not have them compete with workmen already employed; he has the old-fashioned idea of a fixed amount of work to go round. There is no wasting away of population; "the greatest plagues of the city are equally and quickly repaired from the country". It needs only two years to repeople the City after a great Plague; the losses of the City are made good by "new affluxes to London out of the country". The figures show that more people were buried in London than were christened in it.[15] "We may not call that a more sickly year wherein more die, because such excess of burials may proceed from increase and access of people to the City only." Building has decreased in Winchester and Lincoln; London's buildings have actually increased.[16]

"It is certain that London is supplied with people from out of the country, whereby not only to supply the overplus differences of burials abovementioned, but likewise to increase its inhabitants according to the said increase of housing." He says he has ascertained "upon exact inquiry" that there were in the last ninety years 6,339 christenings and only 5,280 burials in the country, leaving, he thinks, a good margin for the country. He supposes in his time a population of 6,440,000 for all England, 460,000 for London and surroundings, or a fourteenth of the whole. Even in the country he thinks he can prove an increase of 600,000 in the forty years after James's accession: "either to render it more populous, or send forth into other colonies or wars".

This "observation" of Graunt adds the definiteness of figures to Harrington's rhetorical description of the relations between City and Country (cf. supra); and there is no such shrewd demographical observation in Harrington to set beside the following in Graunt:[17] "We come to shew why, although in the country the christenings exceed the burials, yet in London they do not. The general reason of this must be that in London the proportion of those subject to die [*sic*] unto those capable of breeding is greater than in the country. That is, let there be an hundred persons in London and as many in the country: we say that, if there be sixty of them breeders in London, there are more than sixty in the country, or else we must say that London is more unhealthful or that it inclines men and women more to barrenness than the country, which, by comparing the burials and christenings of Hackney, Newington, and the other country parishes with the most smoky and stinking parts of the City, is scarce discernible in any considerable degree." He then gives several reasons why the normal results of marriage are hindered in London, the chief being that the nature of London occupations keeps men constantly moving in and out of the City, though one reason is that apprentices marry late, and another is promiscuity and intemperance. The last reason of all, which we may call Herbert Spencer's, is "that the minds of men in London are more thoughtful and full of business than in the country". It is to be remembered that the City of London was still a residential centre, though the palaces had begun to move westward, and "the noblemen's ancient houses are now become Halls for Companies or turned into tenements".[18] Petty thinks the movement was from desire to escape the smoke.

We are no longer in the region of scattered hints. There is a concentration of study on subjects that are the main subjects of demography now. That all Graunt's observations are not equally wise need not surprise us. In two cases perhaps he is deliberately wearing an appearance of unwisdom. In one case, his idea that the moon jerked,[19] when it was only a faulty telescope, he may have known the shortcomings of the telescope. The other is his contribution to the Royal Society's proceedings August 19, 1663; (1) two male and two female carps were put into a new horse-pond at Deptford, and in four years (1658–1662) the carps had increased to 870, and the horses refused to drink; (2) he hears that the length of young salmon was increased by three feet when small pieces of tape were thrust through their gills!

Perhaps these were signs of the dearth of materials which led Halley ten years later to bring forward his very different contribution.

The demographical usefulness of either the carps or the salmon is not evident; of the two the former seems the less trivial. There seems room for fear that Graunt was playing with the Royal Society. If they had not been Graunt's experiments they might not have been noticed at all. An experiment to show that carps can live out of the water on white bread soaked in milk is mentioned by Derham (1711), as described to him "by a person very curious and of great honour and eminence whose word (if I had leave to name him) nobody would question. And it being an instance of the respiration of fishes very singular and somewhat out of the way I have for the reader's diversion taken notice of it".

As Graunt had been dead over thirty years (1674) and was not spoken of with bated breath even during his lifetime, the carps are not his on this occasion; and for introducing them I make the same apology as Derham, of whom more by and by.

There is, I think, no doubt of Graunt's "excellent working head"; but as a demographer he was faced with serious drawbacks. There was no census[20] of the Kingdom; there had been none of the City since 1631. The nearest approach might be the list drawn up for the Poll Tax of 1640. Gregory King was especially good at putting such materials together, but his work seems to have been little known (see Note infra, page 105).

There was a general fear (not only among the Puritans) that to number the people would bring back the Plague as in the time of David.

Graunt, and after him Petty, evaded the prejudice against enumeration by using the roundabout way of Tables of Mortality, not at all a perfect instrument. There was no general practice of registration, though Cromwell had got a law passed for it in 1653. There was no uniform plan of it; and even in London there were notorious gaps, in respect, for example, of Dissenters, not to be filled up by any likely conjecture. Graunt's complacent Anglican orthodoxy amuses us in his tenth chapter, on "Inequality of Parishes". It was soon to give place to a Catholic orthodoxy, which among other things hindered his advancement.

But he is in earnest with his statistics, and deplores the gaps. He dislikes the necessity of saying "a very great number" instead of a precise number, were it only what we call a round one.

Petty himself is said to have chided a member of the Royal Society for saying "considerably bigger" instead of giving "number, weight or measure", and Graunt objected to being told that a death was "of an infant," age not given, or "of an aged person", age not given.[21] "In the matters of infants I would desire but to know clearly what the searchers ["ancient matrons", who report by what disease the corpse died] mean by infants, as whether children that cannot speak, as the word infant seems to signify, or children under two or three years old."—If you are to say the proportion of the "aged" is 15,757 to the total 229,250—that would be of about 1 to 15, or 7 per cent.—"Only the question is what number of years the searchers call aged, which I conceive must be the same that David calls so, viz. Seventy. For no man can be said to die properly of Age who is much less."

It was many centuries before humanity learned to speak in numbers, which are the articulate language of Science. Homer[22] says that Nestor at the Siege of Troy (say 1194 years B.C., its fall being put down for 1184) had lived through "two generations" of men and was beginning a third. Juvenal makes fun of this some 1,200 years after. But it was better than the method of ejaculation: "He was very old." The drawback is we are not told the length of the generation; if we are to add units, they must be similar units. Xerxes, invading Greece, counted his army by putting batches of men successively into an enclosure or pen, which held 10,000, all told, in the case of the first batch; and as he filled the pen 170 times his army was reckoned to have 1,700,000, says Herodotus. Plato does not believe Greek generals could not count even as early as the Trojan War; and Xerxes so long afterwards must have counted the first 10,000 in his pen.

Graunt would have used exact counting if it had been made possible by his data. He avoided most traps; and laid down positions obvious now and novel then. He even gave the first hint, in his eleventh chapter, of the first London Life Table,[23] and was the first to distinguish diseases critically, so as, e.g., to prevent new names being taken for new phenomena, rickets first appearing in 1631, the name being then first given.

Professor Hull sums up the other novelties of Graunt very neatly: The constant relation of chronic diseases, and even common accidents, to the rate of mortality; the excess of male over female births; the high death-rate in the earliest period of life; the excess of the death-rate in the City over that in the Country.

These things were novelties because the Bills of Mortality were a novelty. Paris discovered the wisdom of the practice from Graunt's book, and adopted it in 1667, thereby enabling Graunt in his later editions to compare London and Paris with some certainty. There was a record at Geneva from 1601 which shows a mortality in the first years of life higher than Graunt's for London. But there was no such study of the records there as of the London Bills by Graunt. The closest sequel is Petty's *Observations on the Dublin Bills of Mortality for 1681* (publ. 1683). The most elaborate is much later, Süssmilch's *Göttliche Ordnung*, 1741. There were, besides, practical effects in the improvement of the figures. And this all came from Graunt's having engaged his thoughts, he knew not by what "accident", on a subject which had really engaged his "long and serious perusal". The pamphlet, "not two hours' reading", was worth writing.

Graunt was rather discoverer than inventor; but to his discovery as well as to Petty's inventions we may apply Milton's words: [4]

The inventor all admired, and each how he
To be the inventor missed, so easy it seemed
Once found, which yet, unfound, most would have thought
Impossible.

William Petty, like Richard Lovell Edgeworth, was a born inventor. Son of a clothier in Romsey,

Hampshire, he was born there in 1623. A precocious boy, he early learned Greek and Latin, and also a love of the sea and travel; he early sought out many inventions. The idea of the tanks (of the Great War) is credited to him, as the idea of the bicycle to R. L. Edgeworth. He studied medicine at Leyden, discussed Vesalius' anatomy, and no doubt much else, with Hobbes in Paris, 1645, became teacher of anatomy at Oxford, and then vice-principal of Brasenose, 1648 to 1650, brought a half-hanged woman to life again, and was made by Graunt's influence Professor of Music at Gresham College in 1648 (or perhaps 1646). Music, as we have seen, may have had its Greek sense of Art in general.[25] He became Physician to the Parliamentary Army in Ireland (1652), and for thirty years afterwards that country was the centre of his activities. He made the first thorough survey of Ireland, called the "Down" Survey because *"set down"* in the form of maps! This was finished in four years, 1654 to 1658. It was made in view of Cromwell's Settlement of Ireland in 1652, supposed to begin a new era for the distressful country. We find him in London in 1659 much trusted by Henry Cromwell, Commander of the Irish Forces, and elected for West Looe in Richard Cromwell's Parliament. In earlier years, 1647-8, he had joined several clubs of the *virtuosi* [or fine wits, "highbrows"], including the "invisible" college to which Masson in his Life of Milton traces the Royal Society.[26] He took part also in the discussions of the Rota Club, which met at a coffee-house to debate Harrington's doctrines. Pepys gives us what seems a fair specimen of the debates in his *Diary* of 1659–60.

At the time of his death there was still doubt in some minds whether he was genius or madman.[27] The publication of the *Petty Papers* (1927), giving *inter alia* the draft memoranda of his work, has confirmed the belief that he was near allied to the first. If in spite of the new materials there given we do not attribute *Observations on the London Bills of Mortality* to him, but assign it to Graunt, we still leave him the greater fame than Graunt in popular estimation.

If he had written nothing but the *Taxes and Contributions* he would be one of the chief pioneers of economic study. The *Political Arithmetic* makes him also a pioneer of Statistics. He was conscious that without the basis of actual enumerations his idea of *Political Arithmetic* could not be carried out with confidence. "Without the knowledge of the true number of people as a principle the whole scope and use of the keeping of births and burials is impaired, wherefore by laborious conjectures and calculations to deduce the number of people from the births and burials may be ingenious, but very preposterous."[28] He lamented the gap even for taxation. In practice he attempts to supply the want of a census by calculations, usually multiplications, of figures known to be only roughly accurate. For example, he calculates the population of Ireland from the hearth tax, and there is always a doubt how many heads a hearth implies. We do not add to the accuracy of a figure by multiplying it. The method is really guessing, though the guessing of a shrewd mind, quite likely now and again to be right. We are not getting the statistical warrant for depending on large numbers till we have more than a roughly accurate ascertainment of the large numbers before us. We reason down from them, having obtained them by enumeration, say by a census. Petty in one case is content with one hundred: "By a day's food we understand a hundredth part of what one hundred of all sorts and sizes will eat so as to live, labour and generate." He would need to be sure that his "sample" of a hundred was a fair sample, though this case belongs to a class where guessing may possibly have its chance. To present the numbers of the people, in spite of "David and all his afflictions", nothing will serve us but a census, every five years if possible.

Petty's *Essay on the Future Growth of London* (1682), called *Another Essay* because by an after-thought preceded by one on *The People and Colonies*, has an argument that seems arithmetic, and is really *a priori* economics: "Now whereas in arithmetic out of two false positions the truth is extracted, so I hope out of two extravagant contrary suppositions to draw forth some solid and consistent conclusion." Suppose the City of London seven times bigger than now, suppose it seven times smaller than now—which is the better for our wealth and security? He answers practically that the larger is to be preferred for economy, not only of production, but of government. "Even the arts are best promoted by the greatest number of emulators. And it is more likely that one ingenious curious man may rather be found out amongst 4 millions than 400 persons."

Even in the *Taxes and Contributions* he had written that "fewness of people is real poverty,[29] and a nation wherein are eight millions of people are more than twice as rich as the same scope of land wherein are but four"; the reason was quaint, "for the same governors, *which are the great charge*, may serve near as well for the greater as the lesser number". There seems to him no limit to the numbers supportable by this economy of concentration. He thinks apparently that in England in his time every man had rather too much than too little food, "few men spending less than double of what might suffice them as to the bare necessities of nature". Graunt thought that London without immigration would double in eight times eight years, and in two to five years with it, though he is not careful to be consistent.[30] Petty says the people of London have doubled their number in forty years, and sees no reason "in natural possibility" why it should not happen in ten. It might well happen over the whole kingdom generally in twenty-five if parents were assured of maintenance for their children. Three and a quarter acres of land per head will secure this maintenance, and these are available now in England. It is true that "one acre of land may bear as much corn and feed as many cattle as twenty, by the difference of the soil; some parcel of ground is naturally so defensible as that an hundred men being possessed thereof can resist the invasion of five hundred; and bad land may be improved and made good, bog may by draining be made meadow, heath-land may, as in Flanders, be made to bear flax and clover-grass so as to advance in value from one to an hundred;[31] the same land being built upon many centuple the rent which it yielded as pasture; one man is more nimble or strong and more patient of labour than another; one man by art may do as much work as many without it", as for example if he uses a mill instead of a mortar, or a horse instead of a man's back. "It is hard to say that when these places were first planted whether an acre in France was better than the like quantity in Holland and Zealand; nor is there any reason to suppose but that therefore upon the first plantation the number of planters was in proportion to the quantity of land, wherefore, if the people are not in the same proportion as the land, the same must be attributed to the situation of the land and to the trade and policy of the people superstructed thereupon." He takes the whole problem more lightly than we should now. The main difference seems to be to him situation and ready access to markets. Otherwise to him lands are pretty much alike. "A very little addition to cultivation will produce a fifth more." "Labour is the father of wealth as land is the mother," quoted by Graunt, is a favourite maxim of Petty's. When a man working for himself "hath subducted his seed out of the proceed of his harvest, and also what himself hath both eaten and given to others in exchange for clothes and other natural necessaries, the remainder of corn is the natural and true rent of the land for that year; and the medium of seven years, or rather of so many years as makes up the cycle within which dearths and plenties make their revolution, doth give the ordinary rent of the land in corn". It is rather profit than landlord's rent, which latter is what he calls elsewhere a "superlucration".[32]

"If we consider that England having but three acres to a head as aforesaid, doth so abound in victuals as that it maketh laws against the importation of cattle flesh and fish from abroad, and that the draining of fens, improving of forests, inclosing of commons, sowing of St. Foyne and clover grass be grumbled at by Landlords as the way to depress the price of victuals; then it plainly follows that less than three acres improved as it may be will serve the turn, and consequently that four will serve abundantly."

"Moreover as the inhabitants of cities and towns spend more commodities and make greater consumptions than those who live in wild thin-peopled countries, so when England shall be thicker peopled in the manner before described, the very same

people shall then spend more than when they lived
more sordidly and inurbanely and further asunder
and more out of the sight, observation and emula-
tion of each other, every man desiring to put on
better apparel when he appears in company than
when he has no occasion to be seen." "And now
I shall digress again to consider [in relation to
Ireland] whether it were better for the common
wealth to restrain the expense of 150,000 optimates
below £10 per annum each, or to beget a luxury
in the 950,000 plebeians, so as to make them spend
and consequently earn double to what they at
present do.—To which I answer in brief that the
one shall increase the sordidness and squalor of
living already too visible in 950,000 plebeians with
little benefit to the commonwealth; the other
shall increase the splendour, art, and industry of
the 950,000, to the great enrichment of the common
wealth. Again why should we forbid the use of any
foreign commodity, which our own hands and
country cannot produce, when we can employ our
spare hands and lands upon such exportable commodities as will purchase the same and more?"
This is the standing modern economic argument
for free trade.[33]

Moreover, these passages show that Petty had
a notion of a standard of living. So he says,
"At this day when Ireland was never so rich
and splendid"; yet in the same tract he speaks of
their poorness of living. They live at ease, at too
much ease, because of the potato. In the *Political*

Arithmetic he speaks of the standard of expense, of ordinary English labourers. It seems curious to us that he should think it fostered and preserved by indefinite increase of people. Density of population is a problem presenting many sides, of which he has only seized one. But he is thinking of the problem of government; he is looking at matters from the ruler's point of view, and not much considering the happiness of "the totter-headed multitude". Hobbes swayed him at least as much as Harrington, though with Harrington he thinks "the wealth of the nation is in too few men's hands".

The mere food of the people is always to him the chief necessary, as in the passage from which quotation was made above: "That some men will eat more than others is not material since by a day's food we understand the hundredth part of what one hundred of all sorts and sizes will eat so as to live, labour and generate. And that a day's food of one sort may require more labour to produce than another sort is also not material since [by a day's food] we understand the easiest gotten food of the respective countries of the world." "The day's food of an adult man at a medium and not the day's labour is the common measure of value", and "I valued an Irish cabin at the number of days' food which the maker spent in building of it." He is trying, as he says, to make "a par or equation between lands and labour so as to express the value of anything by either alone".[34] He was struggling with the difficulties that beset Adam Smith, Malthus, and Ricardo in their search for an invariable measure of value. He was not much more unsuccessful than they were. He was successful in improving the statistics of his adopted country.

He was not successful in his best-known scheme for the regeneration of it, which, from his knowledge of its past history, he earnestly desired. His scheme of Transplantation[35] as opposed to Plantation was never taken seriously. It did not mean the transplanting of all the Irish from other counties into Connaught; he opposed that kind of transplantation. It might include the decoying back of the New England settlers, too many of them employed "in the meanest part" of husbandry, the breeding of cattle in patriarchal fashion. "May not the land of superfluous territories be sold, and the peoples with their moveables brought away? May not the English in the America plantations who plant tobacco, sugar, etc., compute what land will serve their turn and then contract their habitations to that proportion both for quantity and quality? As for the people of New England I can but wish they were transplanted into Old England or Ireland according to proposals of their own made within this twenty years although they were allowed more liberty of conscience than they allow one another." At a late period of his life Petty went back to the old plan, and after correspondence with Penn bought land in Pennsylvania and tried to found a little model colony of his own there.

His new plan[36] was mentioned in *Taxes and Contributions*: "Since Ireland is under-peopled in the whole, and since the government there can never be safe without chargeable armies until the major part of the inhabitants be English, whether by carrying over these or withdrawing the other, I think there can be no better encouragement to draw English thither" than to let them know their taxes will be lighter. The plan is most fully described in the *Treatise of Ireland*, 1687, laid before James II, but not published till Hull published it. It is given, substantially, in the *Political Anatomy of Ireland*, 1672 (157–8) and in the *Political Arithmetic*, 1690. In the first it is an exchange of head for head, leaving the numbers the same, "and as many English brought back". In the second and in the *Treatise* (Table 561) it is something different, not an exchange but a subtraction. In the *Political Arithmetic* we are told it is a dream or reverie. Under Catholic James it might be taken more seriously, and Petty increased the transplanted numbers from 200,000 to a million. In the *Political Anatomy* he writes: "If Henry II had or could have brought over all the people of Ireland into England, declining the benefit of their land, he had fortified, beautified, and enriched England, and done real kindness to the Irish. But the same work is near four times as hard now to be done as then; but it might be done even now with advantage to all parties. Whereas there are now 300,000 British and 800,000 Papists, whereof 600,000 live in the wretched way above mentioned—if an exchange was made of but about 200,000 Irish and the like number of British brought over in their rooms, then the natural strength of the British would be equal to that of the Irish, but their political and artificial strength [meaning perhaps industrial] three times as great." If the marriageable women, say 20,000, of the 600,000 were brought over and married to English husbands, and as many English brought over to Ireland to marry Irish husbands, "the whole work of natural transmutation and union would in four or five years be accomplished", and the cabins of the poor Irish would, under their wives' influence, become decent houses. Now, they can run up a cabin in three days, and they live on potatoes and milk; "Why should they desire to fare better, though with more labour, when they are taught that this way of living is more like the Patriarchs of old and the saints of later times . . .? And why should they breed more cattle since it is penal to import them into England?" People say they are thieves, but "thievery is affixt to all thin-peopled countries" without law and order and security. Ireland is a *thin*-peopled country "governed by the laws that were made and first fitted to *thick*-peopled countries".

In the *Political Arithmetic*, Petty, speaking of the relative size and strength of Holland, France, and England, says he has a dream: "If all the moveables and people of Ireland, and of the Highlands of Scotland, were transported into the rest of Great Britain, that then the King and his subjects would become more rich and strong both offensively and defensively than now they are. 'Tis true I have heard many wise men say, when they were bewailing the past losses of the English"—in Irish rebellions over five hundred years—"I have heard wise men in such their melancholies wish that, the people of Ireland being saved, that island were sunk under water. Now it troubles that the distemper of my own mind on this point carries me to dream that the benefit of these wishes may practically be obtained without sinking that vast mountainous island under water, which I take to be somewhat difficult, for although Dutch engineers may drain its bogs, yet I know no artists that could sink its mountains." It would certainly be wicked, perhaps, not to remove mountains, but to take the ground under our feet. The foolish saying (better to sink it under water) has survived to our times when ground is greedily valued. But Petty's own dream was not of submersion but of transplantation. It is true that he would not object to part with the island to a foreign purchaser.[37] But we must take him as standing in the main by his idea of transplantation. He is moved here by all three motives, the political, the economical, and the religious; but the first weighs most—how to make England politically strong; and the other two are subsidiary —how to increase her wealth and how to lessen the weakening influence of religious discord. To raise the condition of the people is nowadays an end in itself; it is not evidently so with Petty, though he is a humane man and a just man, and from time to time he shows his sympathies with the Irish people. He does not propose to make the ransplantation by force as in the case of the conquerors of ancient times, nor even by Act of Parliament, but by a demonstration "that it will be the profit, pleasure, and security of both nations and religions to agree therein".

Suppose all things done as he desires, there would, he estimates, be a million more people in England and a million fewer in Ireland, enough to look after the cattle. The King would do well to buy out the landlords, and the farmers would do well to come over to England; what remains would be, as Lord Lansdowne says, a large cattle ranch. Perhaps the same was intended for Scotland,[38] where he thinks 300 out of 400,000 might be transplanted from the Highlands into the Lowlands. The Dutch, he says, have done well, first in hiring their army from the foreigner and encouraging naturalization, secondly in getting their cattle and corn from the foreigner, viz. the Danes and the Poles, while their own people devote themselves to trade and commerce. What the Dutch do by necessity of situation England might do from choice, throwing up its husbandry and increasing its manufacture and merchandise and carrying trade. In fact, Petty has in this case joined with Harrington, and would like England to "become as it were one city that sucks all the world", or one gigantic workshop. The argument is not very different from Harrington's. The application to Ireland is very different; instead of Petty's transplantation Harrington (in the passage mentioned above) would have a plantation of Jews. In both cases there is an admiration of Holland; but it is not a mere worship of success; it is an approval of Dutch policy founded on a study of the results of it. Sir William Temple, who knew Holland better than either of them, furnishes Petty with one of his points.[39] The Dutch, he says, are forced to their policy. "I conceive the true original and ground of trade to be great multitude of people crowded into small compass of land, whereby all things necessary to life become dear, and all men who have possessions are induced to parsimony, but those who have none are forced to industry and labour or else to want." In Ireland, he says, a man may get in two days' labour enough to feed him for a week, "which I take to be a very plain ground of the laziness attributed to the people". "The want of trade in Ireland proceeds from the want of people", and this from wars and revolutions; so he writes to Essex, 1673. Apart from the wars, he says, "people are multiplied in a country by the temper of the climate favourable to generation, to health, and to long life".

Petty had deplored the fewness of the people in Ireland; his remedy of transplantation would not appear to be any remedy for this particular malady as regards the Irish people left in the country. Even Temple seems to regard the interests of the Irish people as subordinate to the interests of England, and of the English trade, "upon the health and vigour whereof the strength, riches and glory of his Majesty's Crowns seem chiefly to depend". These were the days when Ireland was, on this pretext, denied the English market for her cattle; and Temple is not to blame for the policy in general.

He is said by George Chalmers[40] to have "finely compared" the great body of the people to the base of a pyramid; and the idea has since been used for all manner of purposes which would have very much astonished him. The passage cited is in an essay *On the Original and Nature of Government*, and has not any reflections on a downtrodden multitude such as Chalmers puts into it. Temple is asking himself whether the State would not, like a pyramid, stand more firmly on its base than on its apex. Harrington would have made it rather a globe than a pyramid. Temple, however, was considering things as they are and is dejected about them. Some people in those days became old very early, and Temple had become content in 1673, under fifty, to leave the world as he found it, and when he thought of men like Harrington and Petty, who refused to do so, he observed: "All set quarrels with the Age, and pretences of reforming it by their own Models to Ideal States, end commonly like the pains of a man in a little boat who tugs at a rope that's fast to a ship; it looks as if he resolved to draw the ship to him; but the truth, and his meaning, is to draw himself to the ship, where he gets in when he can and does like the rest of the crew when he is there."

That is to say—general reforms are not to be accomplished without the commandment and will of Princes. In this case Petty tried to win the Princes, without success, and we may wonder at his own belief in his plan. There is nothing absurd in the idea of transplantation to a nation that has gone through so many conquests as the English, involving displacement of old inhabitants and intrusion of new. Some modern schemes of organized emigration are not much less ambitious than Petty's, to say nothing of the deportations of whole nations by Oriental conquerors and the enforced emigrations for conscience' sake familiar to Petty's contemporaries. There was already a drift of English to Ireland at the time. His scale is perhaps too large, and he is trying to turn old countries into new ones in too short a time. His details were criticized carefully by Sir Richard Cox, the contemporary historian of Ireland; Professor Hull quotes many of his shrewd comments. One is on the idea that a million of English women would transform their Irish husbands into Englishmen. No, he said, the husbands would bring them down to their level; better send out English lads who would pick and choose among the Irish women those on their own level; and Cox suggests that it be done year by year. So, when Spain was alarmed lest the depopulation of the home country should be the effect of the withdrawal of so many men to her new colonies, a Spaniard (Uztariz) wrote that you have only to make trade prosperous and the Spanish women will find Catholic husbands, who should be encouraged to come over to share the prosperity.

One interesting feature of Petty's Plan is that he is there trying to improve the quality of the population and raise the Irish standard of comfort to the English. In the legendary story of the Sabine women forcibly married to Roman conquerors in the days of Romulus we know not whether the Roman breed was improved or not.

The Plan of Transplantation was long remembered against Petty. A hundred years and more afterwards, James Anderson, protesting against the crowding of people in cities, wrote that Temple and Petty were strangely dazzled by the precarious prosperity of the Dutch in their day, and Petty had said that "England would be more rich and more powerful, if Scotland, Ireland and Wales were sunk in the sea, provided their inhabitants were first transferred within the bounds of England". Petty had quoted some such saying as this, but not as his own. The same Anderson claims for his own School (of Agriculturists) the maxim which is Petty's—that such inquiries as we now call statistical and economical should keep hold of "number, weight, and measure".[41]

It was a counsel of perfection, "quantitative precision", to be secured wherever we can get it in our data, but a little hazardous sometimes where men are concerned, in our estimate of the future built on the data. Petty has tried to estimate the effects of his plan in quantitative terms that inspire no confidence and not unfrequently baffle his own editors.[42] Professor Hull has noted that Petty's *Arithmetic* was more successful with Taxation and Coinage because it was just there that he found trustworthy figures given by the State to build upon. For a similar building in the case of Population similar accuracy of Tables of Mortality and all other demographical data must lead the way. Efforts like that of Graunt were more valuable than some of Petty's conjectures that seemed accurate because stated in figures, but were not accurate because a sound basis for the figures was wanting. The criticism does not apply merely to the Plan of Transplantation, but to the various estimates of future increase of population in London and in the world in general.

Yet unless we had counsels of perfection we should make no approach to perfection.

RALEIGH TO ARTHUR YOUNG

NOTE I TO CHAPTER III

The *Petty Papers* (*Some Unpublished Writings of Sir William Petty*, edited from the *Bowood Papers* by the Marquis of Lansdowne, 2 vols., 1927) have given to the world a rare opportunity of seeing as it were into the mind of an inventive genius. Here we watch his first trials and clues, pursued or not pursued, for he began far more than he ever worked out; and in theory, except for currency, we have mainly hints. It was with him as with Waring—

> There were sundry jottings,
> Stray leaves, fragments, blurs, and·blottings;
> Certain first steps were achieved.

For example, there is a suggestion of the Germ theory of disease; it is at least as clear as Raleigh's of the Darwinian theory. We cannot, he says, better explain the destruction of so many men by the Plague "than by imagining the same to be done by millions of invisible animals that travel from country to country, even out of Africa into England" (*P.P.*, II. 29). And there is a consciousness of the problem of a Life Table: "The numbers of people that are of every year old from one to a hundred, and the number of them that die at every such year's age do show by how many years' value the life of any person of any age is equivalent, and consequently make a par between the value of estates for life and for years" (*P.P.*, I. 193).

Professor Greenwood, observing more than a consciousness of the problem in the *Discourse concerning Duplicate Proportion*, 1674, discusses the possible service of it in the interpretation of Graunt. See *Statistical Journal*, 1928, Part I, 82. Compare Hull's *Petty*, 622.

NOTE II

Gregory King's *Natural and Political Observations upon the State and Condition of England*, 1696, was till recently known only by the extracts of Charles Davenant (*Balance of Trade*, 1699) and George Chalmers (*Estimate*, 1782, p. 149, and later ed. more fully, as well as in the separate vol. under Gregory King's name in 1810). The manuscript of the whole book was acquired in this century by the Right Hon. John Burns, and is likely to be printed very soon.   101

REFERENCES TO CHAPTER III

1. There is a tract on the subject ascribed to Raleigh, "Causes of the Magnificency and Opulency of Cities" (*Remains*, 1726).

2. *Economic Writings of Sir William Petty*, edited by Dr. C. H. Hull, of Cornell, 2 vols., but paged continuously. Cambridge University Press, 1899. See XXXV, XXXVI and p. 332, also *Petty Papers* (1927), I. XLI, cf. I. xxx.

3. See W. R. Wilde, Assistant Census Commissioner, "Dublin Bills of Mortality", paper read to the Statistical Section of the British Association at Belfast, September 7, 1852, reprinted in *Assurance Magazine*, III. 248–251.

Walloon weavers—Hull, xxxvii.

Petty on Graunt—Hull, 479, 481, 608.

4. *Athenae Oxonienses*, vol. I, 269. So Wood (ib., vol. II. 610, number 511) speaks of Petty's "admirable inventive head".

"Vertuoso"—or "virtuoso" equally common at that time. See *Moral Sense*, p. 49.

"Pettie"—at end, but above "Petty".

5. Authorship, Hull, vol. I. xxxix, 388, cf. Graunt, chap. XII.

6. Argument from obscurity: Shakespeare's Plays could not have been written by an uneducated and unknown man, therefore must proceed from the great Francis Bacon.

7. Professor Major Greenwood, F.R.S., *Statistical Journal*, 1928, Part I, pp. 79 to 85, cf. *Petty Papers*, 1927, vol. II, end.

8. Mr. Henry Higgs, C.B., in *Economic Journal*, 1895, p. 72. Size of City: Hull 321 top, cf. 380, Petty's *Pol. Arith.*, Hull, 505.

9. "Plantation" here from the context must mean cultivation—Hull, 372.

10. Dr. Ogle, *Statistical Journal*, September 1892. "Trustworthiness of the Old Bills of Mortality."

11. Graunt's returns—Hull, 335 ff., 347, 348.

12. Lord Roberts was a Privy Councillor and Lord Privy Seal—Hull, 320, 321.

13. Could turn out thrice as many soldiers as we need.

14. On the inadequacy of his figures, see *Statistical Journal*, 1892, p. 9, Ogle; 1928, Part I. 79, Greenwood; 1928, Part II. 355, Edge. Lump of labour—Hull, II. 353, 354. Waste repaired—ib., 320, 367, 368.

15. The bills record not births, but christenings or baptisms. He deals, however, with births, p. 384.

16. Graunt's, § 4, p. 372 (of Hull), seems to withdraw this argument. Total population of England, Hull, 371.

17. Chapter VI, Hull, 372.

Late marriages, 373.

"Full of business", chap. VII, Hull, 374.

18. Petty, *Taxes*, Hull, 41; cf. Graunt, ib., 380, 394.

19. "The moon jerked"—Hull, 358.

The salmon, ib., 432.

The carps—Derham, *Physico-theology*, 1711, p. 7 note.

20. Census—Hull, 405. Masson, *Life of Milton*, II. 208.

Fate of David's census—Hull, 384, 466, where Hull quotes 2 Samuel xxiv and 1 Chron. xxi.

Registration—Hull, XCI; Graunt, chap. X.

Inequality of parishes—Hull, 382, cf. chap. III, Hull, 355; Suicides, chap. XII. 393. Forced communicants.

Graunt's good intentions—Hull, lxxv, xc, and 362, chap. III. Christenings neglected more than the burials, and are an unsafe guide.

21. Vague numbers—Petty's reproof, Hull, lxiv, cf. 244. Graunt in Hull, 348, 352, cf. 346.

22. Homer, *Iliad*, I. 350. Gladstone, *Primer of Homer* (Macmillan), 46.

Juvenal, X. 246 to 250. Herodotus, VII. 60.

For a discussion of the length of a "generation", see Farr, *Vital Statistics*, 41.

"By fifties in a cave", 1 Kings xviii. 13. Plato crediting the generals with arithmetic, *Republic*, VII. 523.

23. Life Table—See Professor Greenwood, *Statistical Journal*, 1928, Part I, p. 81. See infra (Halley).

Other novelties—Hull, lxxvi.

Paris bills of mortality—Hull, 422.

Geneva—Hull, 386 n. Graunt's seriousness—Hull, 320, 321, 398.

24. Milton, *Paradise Lost*, VI. 498.

25. "Music"—Lansdowne in the *Petty Papers*, I. xxx. Papers XL and XLI are an excellent biography in little.

"Down survey"—*Petty Papers*, vol. I, xvii, cf. xli.

Cromwell's settlement—Hull, 129.

26. Masson, *Life of Milton*, vol. VI, 391, 394; Hull, XXI, cf. XV. Pepys—see note to lecture II. Cf. Masson, V. 481 ff.

27. Petty's talents—Hull, xxix.

New materials—*Petty Papers*, vol. II, 273.

28. "Very preposterous", etc.—*Dublin Bills*, Hull, 485, cf. 491; cf. *Taxes*, ib., 34.

"Roughly accurate"—Hull, lxvii, cf. 619 and 399. The "hundred" —*Pol. Anatomy of Ireland*, in Hull, 181. Another Essay, etc., Hull, 454, cf. 470, 474.

29. In this agreeing with Temple (Sir William), *Works*, I. 6, 110. Petty, *Taxes*, 1662, Hull, 31, 34, cf. 244, 275, 306.

30. Doubling of population—Hull (for Graunt), 388, 394, (for Petty) 459, 462, cf. 468, 603; *Petty Papers*, I. 267, II. 55, 56; cf. Hull, 287.

31. Increasing the fertility. So Professor Cannan contends in the *American Economic Review*, March 1930, p. 78, that land is what man makes it.

The passages in Petty are: *Pol. Arith.*, in Hull, 249, 250, cf. 50, 289.

Labour the father of wealth—Hull, 377, cf. 68.

"Ordinary rent"—*Taxes*, in Hull, 43; more fully in *Anatomy of Ireland*, 180 to 183.

32. "Superlucration"—Hull, 308.

The poor children of Norwich, ages six to ten, earned (in 1671) £1,200 more than they spent, according to Chamberlayne (Edward), *Angliae Notitia*, or Present State of England, Hull, 308. The "super-lucration", or extra-profit, of which Petty expresses no disapproval, was reaped by their parents. There was child-labour before the "Industrial Revolution".

33. Necessaries and luxuries—see *Political Anatomy of Ireland*, 16, 72; Hull, 192, 288 (land necessary).

Free trade, 192.

Standard of living—Hull, 157, 203, cf. 290.

The Potato—Hull, 201, 202; cf. (*Pol. Arith.*) Hull, 306; cf. 181 (food).

"Totter-headed multitude"—Hull (*Taxes*), 23.

Measure of value—Hull, 182.

34. This idea impressed Cantillon, *Nature du Commerce*, 1755, in the passage to which Ad. Smith refers, *W. of N.*, I. viii. 31 (MacC.), Cannan, vol. I. 70.

But see the discussion by Jevons reprinted in *Principles of Economics*, ed. Higgs (Macmillan), 1905, page 168. Compare Petty, in Hull, 181, 182.

35. Transplantation—Hull, 656, 657, cf. 267, 300, 561, liberty of conscience 302.

Pennsylvania—*Petty Papers*, II, sect. XVII, 94 ff., 119 to 121. Compare Hull, 302 n., (*Pol. Arith.*) publ. 1690, but written 1680.

"Proposals"—probably of their English friends in 1650, and refused then. See Hull, 302. Cromwell has the credit of it.

36. "New plan"—Hull, 67, 547, 603, (*Pol. Anat. of Irel.*) 157, 158, (*Pol. Arith.*) 285 ff., (*Taxes*) 60.

"A dream"—(*Pol. Arith.*) Hull, 285.

Seriously—*Petty Papers*, I. 46; Hull, 560, 603, cf. 156 to 158, 202 ft.

"Thin-peopled", etc.—Hull, 202.

RALEIGH TO ARTHUR YOUNG

"Relative size", etc.—Hull, 285, 286.

37. Foreign purchaser—ib. 287.

Cf. the notion that Charles II proposed to sell his rights to Cromwell. Macaulay, *Essays*, II. 82. Davenport (quoting Matthew Paris) says King John was ready to sell "us" to the Moors. "Of Trade", 1700, 78.

"Not by force"—*Treatise of Ireland*, Hull, 561.

Result—Hull, 560, 562; *Petty Papers*, I. 48.

38. Scotland—*Petty Papers*, I. 265, cf. 262; Hull, 287, cf. 266, 267. *Political Arithmetic*, chap. I; Hull, 249 to 268.

39. See Temple's *Essay upon the Advancement of Trade in Ireland*, written to Essex, then Lord-Lieutenant, Dublin, July 22, 1673, in Temple's *Works*, 1720, vol. I, 109 ff. Compare Macaulay's *Essay on Temple*, vol. II, 261, 262 (Methuen's ed., 1903, Notes by F. C. Montague).

Also Temple, *Observations on the United Provinces*, Works, vol. I, chap. VI, contrast with Ireland, 61.

40. George Chalmers, *Estimate of the Comparative Strength of Britain*, 1782, p. 93.

Temple on *Government*, 1673, Works, vol. I, 105.

"A little boat"—Letter to Essex on Ireland, July 22, 1673, Works, vol. II, 121.

Other deportations—For a list, see George Ensor, *Population*, 1818, pp. 180, 225. Another proposal of the kind in the anon. *Letters* concerning the present state of England, 1772, p. 69.

"Drift of English"—Macaulay, l.c. 262.

Cox's criticism—Hull, 158.

Uztariz, *Commercio*, 1724. See Stangeland, *Premalthusian Doctrines of Population*, Columbia Univ. Studies, XXI. 3, 1904, page 171.

Palgr. Dict., new ed., p. 604.

41. James Anderson, *Essential Principles of the Wealth of Nations*, 1797, p. 33, cf. 125; Agriculturists, 56, cf. Hull's *Petty*, 244 (*Pol. Arith.*)

42. "Baffle his own editors"—*Petty Papers*, II. 80, 233, 182, 266 ("totally unintelligible"); Hull, 535, 536, compare LXVII, LXVIII.

IV

HALLEY
(1656–1742)

Of those who helped Demography on its way in those centuries one or two might be reckoned among serious economists, men more or less conscious of a desire to view what we should call the 'economic' situation as a whole, and even to make it a separate study. Such was Charles Davenant (1656–1714), son of the poet supposed to have sheltered Milton. Davenant, in the wake of Petty, wrote on *Ways and Means* (1695) and the *Balance of Trade* (1699). It was he who preserved to us the acute observation of Gregory King (1684–1712) that a short harvest produces a rise in price out of all arithmetical proportion. Tooke states it thus in his second chapter "On Prices": A shortage of one-tenth in the harvest produces an increase in price not of one-tenth but of three-tenths. Sir Matthew Hale was known to Adam Smith at secondhand as a writer under Charles II, who furnished an estimate of the labourer's cost of living in his days.[1] But the memory of those pioneers was more vividly revived a few years after the *Wealth of Nations*, viz. in 1782, when George Chalmers, civil servant, "antiquarian, historian, and economist",[2] found special reason for reviving it. To dispel the general despondency and belief in Britain's decadence he published in that year his "*Estimate of the Comparative Strength of Britain during the Present and Four Preceding Reigns*,[3] to which is added an Essay on Population by the Lord Chief Justice Hale".[4] What Chalmers calls an essay is simply the tenth chapter of Hale's second section, entitled "Moral Evidences concerning the Origination of Mankind", faithfully transcribed by Chalmers from p. 225 to p. 238, with the omission of the Jewish history. Chalmers finds more in Hale than this essay to fortify his estimate, Hale having fortified his own thesis (that population is not eternally constant but is always growing) by Graunt's *Observations*. Hale says: "And because that there can be no greater evidence of this truth of the increase of mankind than experience and observation, neither can there be any observation or experience of greater certainty than the strict and vigilant observance of the calculations and registers of the bills of births and deaths, and because I do not know any one thing rendered clearer to the view than this gradual increase of mankind by the curious and strict observations of a little pamphlet entitled *Observations upon the Bills of Mortality*, lately printed, I shall not decline that light or evidence that this little book affords in this matter, wherein he plainly evinceth"—what we already have seen in Graunt's book of 1662. Hales adds: "These are some of those plain and evident observations of the seemingly inconsiderable pamphlets [Dublin bills included], which give a greater demonstration of the gradual increase of mankind upon the face of the earth than a hundred notional arguments can either evince or confute, and therefore I think them worthy of being mentioned to this purpose."

"And let any man but consider the increase of

London within the compass of forty or fifty years, we shall according to the observations framed to my hands find that the in-parishes until the late fire (1666) in that time have increased from nine to ten or a tenth part and that the sixteen out-parishes have in that time increased from seven to twelve and yet without any decrement or decay of the rest of the kingdom."

Yet if any nation has had experience of plagues, wars, shipwrecks, "we more". And we have sent troops abroad, and we have transplanted numbers into settlements abroad. Notwithstanding all these "correctives" our numbers have increased, and Hale believes the same is true of other nations, "the multitude of them, that are born and live, over-balance the number of them that die, *communibus annis*, or being taken upon a medium".

Botero had thought, on the contrary, that for 3,000 years the numbers had been always at their maximum, which implies no very sanguine view of human resources, or of our success in crowding out the animals. Hale does not in so many words assert that the growth of the numbers has depended on the growth of resources, but makes it clear that he would not have used the expression of a contemporary Josiah Child: "most nations in the civilized parts of the world are more or less rich or poor proportionably to the paucity or plenty of their people and not to the sterility or fruitfulness of their lands".[5] Child is usually more careful, and he is one of those who heartily recognized "the most industrious English calculator this age has produced in public, Captain Graunt" (ib., 191). Chalmers, looking back a hundred years, speaks as if Graunt got little recognition and little help; "unfortunately Graunt's correspondents were not actuated by his ardour". This seems hard, for Petty was among them. But there is at least a laudable admiration of Graunt. Chalmers, taking as his own criterion of English prosperity the tonnage of ships and entries of customs, the ledger of imports and exports (chap. 35), can say no better for it than what (he says) Hale said of Graunt's record of parish registers, "that it gives a greater demonstration than a hundred notional arguments can either evince or confute".

Halley does not receive the same attention from Chalmers, or, so far as I have observed, any attention at all. But his part was nearly as great.

The men who did most for Demography in those days were not in England at least the economists, or embryo economists, but all sorts and conditions of thinking men. Graunt was the City magnate; Halley was the distinguished astronomer, the finder of Halley's comet, one day to be Astronomer Royal. He was born in East London in 1656, and died in 1742 at Greenwich. He was only thirty-seven when in 1693 he used Graunt's example (in his eleventh chapter) and Justell's data to frame the first Life Table. He applied it, from whose example if anyone's might be debatable, to Life Annuities, then likely to be a topic of public interest. Certainly the Royal Society had every reason to be grateful to him, if he succeeded in clearing up this problem also.

The idea that "expectation of life" varies with age is so familiar to ourselves that everyone who goes to insure his life is prepared to be asked how old he is and to pay a high or low premium accordingly.

But life insurance was little known in the seventeenth century, indeed thought hardly right. In France the prejudice against it lasted in some quarters to the end of the eighteenth century. Émerigon, who writes in 1783 on insurance, says that life insurance is allowed in Naples, Florence, and England, but not in France, and that, he says, is quite right, for, he says, "man is beyond price" —the life of man should not be an object of trade or wager—what you improperly call insurances are just wagers.[6] The same prejudice had led to the old argument that the human body was too sacred to be a subject of anatomy, man being an end in himself. England held out against a census longer than against human anatomy or life insurance. We might have expected as strong a prejudice to exist against life tables; Derham and Süssmilch, however, had placed theology on their side by their appeal to final causes and divine order; and they adopted the idea at once.

Societies for life insurance had arisen in the middle of the seventeenth century on the principle of mutual liability; a group of persons forming the society insured each other, and on the occurrence of a death each member paid a fixed contribution. Age was not regarded. That at the end of the century age came to be regarded was due on the Continent to De Witt, and in England to Edmund Halley, famous in Science as De Witt in Politics, not like Graunt, a man from whom nothing could be expected. Graunt held on his way; his facts carried him, some said, better than any "notional arguments", but when the notional argument or principle appeared in Pascal and Halley it seemed to be as much in the nature of things as the "facts" unillumined by the dangerous notional idea of Probability.

This is how Halley found opportunity to give the illumination.[7] The Royal Society in the second decade of its existence found its supply of "transactions" running short, and publication was stopped for a year or two. Rather than have it stopped any longer Halley and a few others undertook to find papers; and, looking out for promising subjects, Halley was struck by a communication furnished by Mr. Justell, a correspondent of his, and proceeding from Dr. Neumann, of Breslau; Halley noticed that it gave not only births and deaths, but, what was not in Graunt's data, *ages* of those dying; and the idea seems then to have struck him of a real Life Table. His data were thus better than Graunt's, though the ages of the living, which a census would give, were still wanting.

As far as England is concerned Halley is so

important that the title of his paper of 1693 contributed to the Royal Society must be given in full: *"An Estimate of the Degrees of the Mortality of Mankind drawn from curious Tables of the Births and Funerals at the City of Breslau, with an attempt to ascertain the Price of Annuities upon Lives. By Mr. E. Halley, R.S.S. [Regiae Societatis Secretarius]."*[8]

Here follows the first two paragraphs: "The contemplation of the Mortality of Mankind has, besides the moral, its physical and political uses, both of which have been some years since most judiciously considered by the curious Sir William Petty in his *Natural and Political Observations on the Bills of Mortality of London,* owned by Captain John Graunt: And since in a like treatise on the Bills of Mortality of Dublin. But the deduction from those bills of mortality seemed even to their authors to be defective: First, in that the number of the people was wanting [there was no census]. Secondly that the ages of the people dying was not to be had. And lastly that both London and Dublin by reason of the great and casual accession of strangers who die therein (as appeared in both by the great excess of the funerals above the births) rendered them incapable of being standards for this purpose, which requires, if it were possible, that the people we treat of should not at all be changed but die where they are born, without any adventitious increase from abroad or decay by migration elsewhere."

"This defect seems in a great measure to be

satisfied by the late curious tables of the bills of mortality at the city of Breslau, lately communicated to this Honourable Society by Mr. Justell, wherein both the ages and sexes of all that die are monthly delivered and compared with the number of births for five years last past, viz. 1687–88–89–90–91, seeming to be done with all the exactness and sincerity possible.''

Breslau is on the Oder, far inland, with a settled population at that time, Halley says, of about 34,000, devoted to linen manufacture, with little efflux or influx of people. Halley regrets the absence of a census, but infers the numbers from the excess of births above deaths. He regrets that he has only five years of record; and makes at least one correction by "our own experience in Christ Church Hospital", Bluecoat School, where, the ages being fourteen to seventeen, "there die of the young lads much about one per cent per annum".

"From these considerations I have formed the adjoined table whose uses are manifold and give a more just idea of the state and condition of mankind than anything yet extant that I know of. It exhibits the number of people in the city of Breslau of all ages from the birth to the extreme old age, and thereby shows the chances of mortality at all ages, and likewise how to make a certain estimate of the value of annuities for lives which hitherto has been only done by an imaginary valuation; also the chances that there are that a person of any age proposed does live to any other age given, with many more, as I shall hereafter show." Here is one of the many more (289–90): "By what has been said the price of insurance upon lives ought to be regulated, and the difference is discovered between the price of insuring the life of a man of twenty and fifty. For example it being a hundred to one that a man of twenty dies not in a year, and but thirty-eight to one for a man of fifty years of age."

"On this depends the valuation of annuities upon lives, for it is plain that the purchaser ought to pay for only such a part of the value of the annuity as he has chances that he is living; and this ought to be computed yearly, and the sum of all those yearly values being added together will amount to the value of the annuity for the life of the person proposed."

It will occur to most of us that if London was too bad for a standard of the values of life at different ages Breslau was too good. And this occurs to Halley himself near the end of his paper:

"It may be objected that the different salubrity of places does hinder this proposal from being universal; nor can it be denied. But, by the number that die being 1,174 per annum in 34,000, it does appear that about a 30th part die yearly, as Sir William Petty has computed for London, and the number that die in infancy is a good argument that the air is but indifferently salubrious [in Breslau]. So that by what I can learn there cannot perhaps be one better place proposed for a standard. At least it is desired that, in imitation hereof, the curious in other cities would attempt something of the same nature, than which nothing perhaps can be more useful" (299–300).

If we had ideal men and ideal conditions of life, what is their Table of Mortality, for as we now conceive him even the Ideal Man must die sometime? *Omnia mors poscit; Lex est, non poena, perire.*[9] The question reminds us of the way Malthus approached his subject at the beginning of the Essay. He is always trying to bring out the difference between a tendency to increase and an actual increase. Look where we like we find no actual instance of a population subject to no checks at all and increasing *ad libitum.* But Malthus takes the case of the American Colonies, an actual instance, where the checks count for so little that we come near the absence of them imagined in our first abstraction. In taking the American Colonies we are taking an instance that would be declared by critics far too good, as London would have been far too bad. But, if you are able to explain why the one is so much more good than the other, as Breslau than London, and especially if you can procure a chain of such tables and reports, you help us to understand the intermediate cases— lying shall we say between Breslau and London.

Dr. Farr in our own day drew up a "Healthy District Life Table",[10] based on returns for five years, 1849–1853, from sixty-three English districts where the mortality did not exceed 17 per thousand persons living in 1841 to 1850. It represented (he said) "a standard of *attained* healthiness; it is impossible to say how much it is below an *attainable* standard". No doubt Mr. Edwin Chadwick would have said "very much below"; but it is a valuable approximation.

It has been a criticism or comment made not only on Halley's Table, but on every such—that it represents a stationary population, the births equal to the deaths, and there being neither immigration nor emigration. Dr. Farr remarks this of the Carlisle table of Milne, and adds: "All correct life tables are constructed on the same hypothesis and therefore admit of comparison." As the figures supplied by the Bills of Mortality or the present-day Registers are by no means in accordance with any such theory, they require an *adjustment*. Dr. Farr induces a scientific parallel. "The adjustment, which makes a life table represent as nearly as possible the progress of the human generation year by year through life, has been employed upon the same principle that astronomers reduce all their observations both of right ascension and declination to some common and convenient epoch. By correcting or equating the observation of earth's axis for *nutation* is always understood in astronomy the getting rid of a periodical cause of fluctuation, and presenting a result not as it was observed but as it would have been observed had that cause of fluctuation had no existence." This adjustment, now a permanent possession, was not Halley's, but is in the spirit of Halley.

That men had not till those days any theory of Probabilities is far from meaning that they had no words for probable and improbable. It seems to us nowadays so evident that vital statistics and a theory of Probabilities must go together that we are surprised to find nothing of the sort in Graunt and Petty. Surely, we might think, the idea of chance and the idea of probability are at least "half as old as time". Yes; but you do not expect the theory of the composition of the air or the theory of the tides to be known by everyone who speaks of the air and the tides. In England there was hardly any recognition of probabilities of life as subject of a theory before Halley introduced it in the paper just quoted; and the idea did not "set the Thames on fire" when he did this.

The general reflections with which Halley concludes his famous paper are hardly so valuable as the rest of it. It is possible that he had been a little influenced by Hale, but there is a touch of Harrington. He says that his table shows 7,000 women between sixteen and forty-five, of whom, were they all married, four out of six should bring a child every year, whereas only one in six does so. There might be four times as many births as now. There is no cause for this in the nature of the species. The reason is that people fear to marry "from the prospect of the trouble and charge of providing for a family", and this is due to "the unequal distribution of possessions, all being necessarily fed from the earth, of which yet so few are masters. So that besides themselves and families, they are yet to work for those who own the ground that feeds them. And of such does by very much the greater part of mankind consist; otherwise it is plain that there might well be four times as many births as we now find." The glory of a King is in the multitude of his subjects. Celibacy ought to be discouraged and taxed, bounties might be given to large families (on the principle of *jus trium liberorum*).[11] "But especially by an effectual care to provide for the subsistence of the Poor by finding them employments whereby they may earn their bread without being chargeable to the Public."

These ideas are less fruitful as well as less novel than those on the Life Table. Halley's aim in the last was (1) to improve Graunt's figures by bringing Breslau to the help of London, (2) to give a scientific basis for Life Annuities. Graunt had not touched the latter subject. But twenty-two years before Halley touched it, John de Witt had discussed it, with Pascal behind him; and had drawn up proposals. A strange oblivion settled down on the proposals after the violent death of de Witt in 1672. They certainly could not have been, like Mendelism, obscured by the obscurity of the author. They were simply pigeon-holed among State papers, still known by report to a few, but sought for by outsiders[12] in vain, till in our own time, in the year 1851, they were published by the energy and pertinacity of a well-known statistician, Frederick Hendriks, actuary of the Globe Insurance Company. He printed them in the *Assurance Magazine*, and also reprinted them for private circulation in a little volume of two parts. The title of both was as in the *Magazine*: *Contributions to the History of Insurance and of the Theory of Life Contingencies, with a restoration of the Grand Pensionary de Witt's Treatise on Life Annuities.*

De Witt was anxious to raise money for the States at a time (1671) when the French were over-running the country and money was sorely needed. Hitherto Life Annuities, as distinguished from redeemable or perpetual, had been granted on far too easy terms; young lives and old were hardly distinguished. Now De Witt appeared on the scene with treasurer Hodde, a good mathematician, to help him. They employed Pascal's new idea of a calculus of probabilities, and are said by Mr. Hendriks to have used parish records of mortality.[13] What is certain is that they drew up a statement for their Cabinet of their case for such a reform of the life annuities as should make these annuities more profitable to the State. They stated their points with painful simplicity, knowing their men and their men's unfamiliarity not only with the higher but with the lower mathematics. The two heroes convinced their superiors, but the matter went no further, in those sad times.

It was remarked above that they had Pascal behind them. Blaise Pascal (1623–1662), of the

Convent of Port Royal, is associated by many of us, from our youth upwards, with crushing replies to what by a curious coincidence was called *Probabilism*, a shelter of the Jesuits in cases of moral difficulty, the replies being set down at large in the *Letters to a Provincial from a friend in Paris*, 1656. How came he to discuss scientific probability? There was no doubt of his powers; he was in the foremost rank of mathematicians; but he was supposed to be buried in Theology.

It is said that about 1654 his friend De Méré, whose studies were but little on the Bible, and who loved dice and betting, drew him into a discussion of the doctrine of chances. You will find the story in the works of the great Leibnitz, in his Reply to Bayle's strictures on his *Nouveaux Essais*, 1702. As given by Erdmann,[14] the story lacks the lively circumstantial details of Hendriks' version. Otherwise the original is racier than the translation. Pascal's own version of his conclusions was not printed till 1679, in his letters to Fermat.

But his views had been, before then, taken up and expounded by Christian Huygens at the time, and Francis Schooten in 1657. It was as if Pascal had stooped for a minute or two by chance over the theory of chances, had solved the problem in principle, left the details to others, and then plunged again into theology.

What concerns us is his indirect influence on the whole course of vital statistics.[15] If, like Pascal, Halley helped us only once, our gratitude is great to both; but Halley worked out a sample lesson for us that we could follow; Pascal does not seem to have done even that. Huygens and he "worked out a few simple exercises" in the problems of gaming; then Bernoulli extended the "principle of indifference", as Mr. Keynes calls it, into the Law of Great Numbers.

Pascal's principles laid hold on De Witt and Hodde; and happily were not pigeon-holed with De Witt's papers; it is more than likely that they had spread to England and become known to Halley by 1693. We read in Halley's paper of "the *odds* that there is that a person of that age does not die in a year"—again "it is *an even lay* at what age a person of any age shall die", "this calculus", etc. It is true that he was only using the common language of betting.

We are all indebted to Dr. William Farr for pointing out that Addison's "Visions of Mirzah" in No. 159 of the *Spectator*, 1711, are a reminiscence of Halley's Life Table. Addison, who was born in 1672 (and died in 1719), might quite well in his twenty-first year have heard of the appearance of the Table, 1793. Most of us, before or after our twenty-first year, have read "the Visions"—the bridge of this life with its threescore and ten arches, the varying fortunes of those who cross or fail to cross them, the dark cloud at each end, the hidden pitfalls set very thick at the entrance of the bridge, so that throngs of people no sooner break through the cloud than many fall into the pitfalls, the pitfalls growing thinner towards the middle, but multiplying and lying closer together towards the end of the arches left entire. It is a lovely commentary on the Life Table; and Mirzah's shepherd-guide or genius might have drawn out the idea of the pitfalls besetting human life and further illustrated the science without injuring the poetry.

This further illustration has been finely done in a picture to be found in the Galtonian Laboratory; and the picture is finely expounded in Professor Karl Pearson's address on the "Chances of Death".

From the plural of his title (Visions) Addison seems to have projected a second Vision. It is clear to all who read his first from end to end that it was written for its moral lessons, not for any scientific purpose. Each of us in the course of the years is struggling across one or other of those arches; let us remember our latter end, which may come soon or late. The Visions are like a Platonic myth at the end of a dialogue, where there usually was one with its moral.

It does us nothing but good to see such pictures. But the apparatus of the demographer on working days, like the apparatus of the medical man, is prosaic and intellectual. We can hardly think of the study of vital statistics without its large array of indispensable tools. The tools have grown with the work. The first of them was the human Language, without which all our thoughts would be beyond the reaches or at least the grasp of our own souls, and beyond even the reaches of other souls than our own. Then we need an Arithmetic that goes beyond the fingers. We must have a Census, and we must have a Registration of births, marriages, and deaths; we must have a Life Table and some sort of doctrine of Probabilities. At the beginning of our seventeenth century there was a mere endeavour after *some* of these. The end of the century saw the need of *all* acknowledged, and it saw some of them accomplished.

APPENDICES TO CHAPTER IV

I

In the *Statistical Journal*, 1928, p. 83, Professor Greenwood finds the skeleton of a life table in Graunt's eleventh chapter; "Of the number of inhabitants", the table itself in section nine (Hull, II. 386).

"Whereas we have found that of one hundred quick conceptions [as opposed to stillborn] about thirty-six of them died before they be six years old and that perhaps but one surviveth seventy-six, we, having seven decades between six and seventy-six, we have sought six mean proportional numbers between sixty-four, the remainder living at six years [100—36] and the one which survives seventy-six, and find that the numbers following are practically near enough to the truth, for men do not die in exact proportions nor in fractions: from whence arises this Table following:

Viz. of an hundred there die within the first six years	36.
the next ten years or decad	24.
the second decad	15.
the third decad	9.
the fourth	6.
the next	4.
the next	3.
the next	2.
[100]....................	1.

[Section] 10
From whence it follows that of the said hundred conceived, there remain alive

at six years end	64.
at sixteen years end	40.
at twenty-six	25.
at thirty-six	16.
at forty-six	10. [9].
at fifty-six	6.
at sixty-(six)	3. (4).
at seventy-six.................	1. (2).
at eighty-(six) ....,,,,,,,	0,

(Section) 11. It follows also that of all which have been conceived there are now alive forty per cent above sixteen years old, twenty-five above twenty-six years old sic deinceps as in the above Table. There are therefore of aged between sixteen and fifty-six the number of forty less by six viz. thirty-four, of between twenty-six and sixty-six the number of twenty-five less by three viz. twenty-two et sic deinceps". "It is clear", says Professor Greenwood (loc. cit.), "that the author had grasped the fundamental idea of a life table". Elsewhere Graunt makes approach to a doctrine of probabilities in a facetious passage of his chapter III § 12. "I dare insure any man, at this present well in his wits, that he shall not die a lunatic in Bedlam within these seven years because I find not above one in about one thousand five hundred have done so" (Hull, II. 355).

II

Tetens (Professor J. N.), writing on Annuities in 1785, says confidently: "Huygens before him had taught how to compute probabilities. His principles Halley applied to the registers of death, when they were brought into order and formed the method upon which to compute Life and Widows' Annuities. Some still call such method 'Halley's.'" (Quoted by Hendriks, *Assurance Magazine*, I. 1850, p. 14, note No. 2). Tetens adds it is not "Halley's method" but "nature's method". Tetens had written on philosophy (1780, "Metaphysics") and like Boyle on natural theology ("Proofs of the Being of a God," 1761). He could hardly have paid Halley a greater compliment, and he knew what he was saying.

Professor Karl Pearson doubts if Halley owed anything to Huygens.

III

KERSSEBOOM

The improvement of Graunt's figures was carried further by a countryman of De Witt, Willem Kersseboom (1691–1771). Like Graunt, though in higher spheres, he used his official opportunities for the benefit of vital statistics. At various times in his life he held important diplomatic and financial appointments under the Dutch Government. There was then no census; but he arrived at the life table for Holland, first, by using parish records in the manner in which Graunt used the Bills of Mortality—for the earlier ages; in the second place, for the later ages, the more accurate and detailed figures within his ken officially—viz. those relating to life annuitants, all naturally of the higher ages. Perhaps for ordinary folk the most intelligible account of his labours is that of Dr. Lippert, then Librarian of Statist. Bureau, Berlin, in Conrad's *Handwörterbuch der Staatswissenschaften* (1890 seq.), pp. 669–71. He is there described as the first to introduce political arithmetic into Holland; and it is true he himself uses the phrase in *Proeven van politique rekenkunde*, 1748, for the title of one of his books, as did Arthur Young at the end of the century. We might describe him as the father of Dutch vital statistics or demography, terms conveying to most of us a more definite and concrete meaning than political arithmetic. (But cf. *Palgrave's Dict. Arithmetic Political.*)

In any case a life table, so drawn up from those two sources, was made by him in 1738 a basis for a calculation of the total numbers of the people, on the assumption of a stationary population. Statisticians tell us that this assumption is hazardous, for "in an increasing population the average age at death is less [there being more young people] and the annual mortality less than in a stationary population having the same expectation of life" (Milne *apud* Farr, l.c. 457), and that life tables must not be founded on tables of mortality alone (ib., 456). Kersseboom seems to have been quite aware of the trap (see Lippert, 670, 1).

Having reached his total 980,000, he finds it is related to the included yearly births as one to thirty-five. Hence his dictum: "A country has thirty-five times as many inhabitants as its yearly births". His numerous critics, English, French, and German, as well as Dutch, did not reject the formula because it was a formula. Struyck, his countryman, would make the relation one to thirty, and use that formula instead. Some such idea prevailed elsewhere. In Adam Anderson's well-known *Historical and Chronological Deduction of Commerce*, four quarto vols., 1787, commonly called *Anderson on Commerce*, we read in volume III. 235, year 1742, that some one estimated the population of Dublin at 76,560, because that figure came out if you multiply the burials by thirty-three—the editor commenting "provided the numerous papists of that city and all the protestant dissenters do duly register their burials, which at least is doubtful". This is hardly an objection on principle.

Later (ib., 317) in 1760 the population of Dublin was found to be 94,227, "which by no means agrees", says Anderson, "with the generally received rule of multiplying the total number of persons dying annually by thirty-three, if in small and healthy places, or in the open country—or by thirty if in great cities where debauchery and the use of spirituous liquors are prevalent". The writer doubts the accuracy of bills of mortality, not only here but elsewhere. The calculation at one to thirty is drawn out more elaborately for cities (376).

Busching, one of Kersseboom's critics, had used this "rule of thumb" to arrive at the population of Silesia (Anders, ib., 430).

Abraham De Moivre (1667–1754), writing on Life Annuities in 1724, had proposed to shorten calculation by assuming that after twelve years of age the numbers living decreased in arithmetical progression—by equal decrements—till all were gone at eighty-six, which he thought the limit of life. Dr. Farr (l.c., 464) says that few errors result in practice from the adoption of this rule. However we read in *Encycl. Brit.*, 1824, vol. I. 368, in the well-known article by Joshua Milne, the introducer of the Carlisle Life Table, 1776–1851, that, though the results were good between thirty and seventy, the general effect of De Moivre's authority was to weaken the efforts of inquirers to find the best life table.[1]

Kersseboom from his official position in the Finance department could hardly have been unaware of De Witt's proposals of 1671, and he worked with great industry at both of Halley's problems. Witness the list of Kersseboom's books, e.g. *Lottery loans*, 1737; *Numbers of the people of Holland*, 1738, 1742;

---

[1] Cf. F. Y. Edgeworth's account of De Moivre in *Palgrave's Dict.*, vol. I. 545, where the reference should read: "Farr, *Vital Statistics*, 1885, p. 464", and not as in my friend's text.

Political Arithmetic (Rekenkunde), 1748, applied to numbers of the people, widows' expectation of life, advantage of life annuities over redeemable, etc.

Besides his great controversies with Simpson, Struyck, John De Witt, Burch, he had a small one with Johann Peter Süssmilch, of whom more will be heard by and by; but in essentials Süssmilch and Kersseboom were in agreement. Thomas Simpson was the author of a *Doctrine of Annuities and Reversions*, 1742,[1] when there was controversy over the new materials provided for London, in the path of Graunt's inquiries, by William Maitland. Maitland had furnished figures of London mortality for ten complete calendar years, 1728–1737 inclusive.[2] Out of these figures Kersseboom framed a table of "values" in Halley's sense, on a wider basis than Halley's, but still on the assumption of a stationary population. It became known as Kersseboom's Table of London Mortality.[3]

Maitland's results enabled Kersseboom to show that Graunt's disproportion of male to female births, fourteen to thirteen,[4] should read eighteen to seventeen. Both men were aware that the balance was reversed by the vicissitudes of life in the later ages of it. It was well to make it clear that even in Vital Statistics the difference of the sexes is not entirely negligible (cf. Farr, 145). Malthus[5] is startled to find the Russian figures and the Swedish at variance in regard to female mortality.

Light was thrown on the same subject by *Deparcieux* (Antoine, 1703-1768), a humble French peasant and a born mathematician. He published in 1746 his *Essai sur les probabilités de la durée de la vie humaine*, with two new life tables, one

---

[1] Praised by Milne, *Encycl. Brit.*, l.c.
[2] *History of London*, 1739. See Farr, l.c. 145.
[3] Lippert, *Handwörterb*, sub voce.
[4] Hull, 374–6 (Graunt, chap. VIII. Lippert's printer on p. 670 inverts Graunt's figures). Cf. Farr, *Vital Statistics*, 104. The difference between $1 : 1\frac{1}{13}$ and $1 : 1\frac{1}{17}$ becomes great with great numbers.
[5] Malthus, *Essay*, second edition, 214–15, on the Russian paradox. Cf. *Malthus and his Work*, 133 ft.

from the figures for French Tontine insurance and one from Monasteries and Nunneries. The latter brought out the greater longevity of the nuns as compared with the monks. He made separate life tables for them and found the *vie moyenne* of the nuns the greater (*Palgrave's Dict., Deparcieux,* by F. Y. Edgeworth).

Our friend Edgeworth rightly identifies Deparcieux with the *geomètre* of the dialogue in Voltaire's *L'homme aux quarante écus* (1768, Genève), where he is described as having written on the length of human life and on Annuities (p. 9, cf. 23 *Calcul des probabilités*). The passage is not only witty, but in surprisingly good taste. The great Buffon also made a Life Table.

IV

Mirzah's Vision Reinterpreted

See Professor Karl Pearson's *Chances of Death; Studies in Evolution,* Essays in two volumes (Arnold), 1897—volume I, pp. 29 to 37, compare 8 to 11 and 25. The frontispiece of the volume is a reproduction of this adapted Vision of Mirzah. The following interpretation owes much to Miss Elderton, of the Galtonian Laboratory.

Death is attacking the living column crossing the Bridge of Life. He makes use of several marksmen aiming with different degrees of precision and different skewness of aim at different portions of the column. At each step men may be hit by more than one marksman, for, though the marksmen aim at one portion of the column passing over the bridge, they may hit another.

One particularly fatal marksman (1) aims at the age of seventy-two, but the mean of his hit is in the sixty-seventh year; he is a very destructive marksman armed as it were with a rifle. Another (2) aims at the forty-second year; he hits only one hundred and seventy-three, of a thousand who started at the bridge, as compared with the four hundred and eighty-four killed by the rifleman; his fire is slow and scattered, and his work might be typified by a blunderbuss. A third (3) aims at the twenty-third year; the total number of deaths due to this marksman is small; the small mortality of youth might be typified by giving Death a bow and arrow. (4) The maximum deadliness is in the third year of life, but the mean age is at six for the mortality of childhood. There is much more concentrated fire; the deadliness of the marksman who aims at the children is nearly three and a half times as great as that of him who aims at youth. His weapon is more like the machine gun than the bow. (5) In the mortality of infancy—the marksman combines intense concentration and extreme deadliness; his blow is dealt alike at antenatal and postnatal life. Bad parentage must be the source of this high mortality—the marksman strikes down with the bones of the ancestry—hence the skull in the picture.

Professor Karl Pearson tells us that he first thought of such a picture in 1875 when looking at Holbein's "Dance of Death" (*Essay*, I, p. 8). This first essay, on the Chances of Death, was given as a lecture at Leeds, 1895. "It would need a great artist to bring that human procession vividly before the reader. Such alone could fully realize my dream on the Mühlenbrücke at Luzern of twenty years ago. But I ventured to put the roughest of sketch suggestions before two artists. The one, trained in the modern impressionist school, failed, I venture to think, in fully grasping the earnestness of life; the other reared among the creations of Holbein, Flaxman, and Blake, shows more nearly the spirit of my dream (see frontispiece)" (I. 40).

The procession, of one thousand living (I. 25), including antenatal nine months, is distinguished into five "ages" of life (l.c., 28 seq.), not seven, as in *As You Like It*. So in vol. I. 124 (*Socialism and Natural Selection*) Mortality at different ages, typical of civilized man, is so set forth:—

Old age centring about......	67..........	484	
Middle life	41..........	173	out
Youth	22..........	51	of
Child	6..........	46	1,000
Infancy..................	2..........	246	

(Antenatal 9 months, add 200).

RALEIGH TO ARTHUR YOUNG

REFERENCES IN CHAPTER IV

1. *Wealth of Nations*, I, VIII. 35, where Davenant and Gregory King are also mentioned.
2. Professor Gonner in *Palgrave's Dict.*, art. "George Chalmers". Chalmers was born 1742, died 1823. Compare above, p. 108.
3. The reigns were of William, Anne, George I, II, III, so far as the last had gone.
4. *The Primitive Origination of Mankind considered and examined according to the Light of Nature.* Written by the Honourable Sir Matthew Hale, Knight, late Chief Justice of his Majesties' Court of King's Bench, London. Printed by William Godbid for William Shrowsbury at the Sign of the Bible in Duke Lane, 1677. Folio. Pp. 380 + Preface to the Reader, pp. 4. Portrait as frontispiece. Hale, born in 1609, died in 1676; the publication was therefore posthumous.
   Graunt *apud* Hale, sect. II, chap. VIII, p. 205, 206, cf. 190, 189, and Graunt's chapters VIII, XI, XII.
5. Child, *Discourse of Trade*, 1698, p. 179, on Graunt, 191. Chalmers, *Estimate* 109, cf. chap. XXXV and p. 52.
6. Hendriks in the *Assurance Magazine*, II, 1852, p. 230, in reprint 38.
7. For Graunt's nearest approach—see appendix to this chapter. For Tetens' commentary see Part II of Appendix.
   Compare *Assurance Mag.*, vol. I, *History of Assurance* by E. J. Farren, 40 to 46, who appeals to Weld's *History of the Royal Society*, I. 326.
8. *Miscellanea Curiosa*, 1705 (p. 282), in the Library of the Royal Statistical Society, presented by Professor Udny Yule.
   The following extracts are from that edition in the following order: 288, 285, 286, 289, 290, 299, 300. Cf. Hull, 535, from Petty, *Pol. Ar.*, 1687.
9. Death claims everything. To pass away is a law, not a penalty. Seneca.
10. Malthus' *Essay* (quarto, 1803), 2nd ed., pp. 4 ff. Farr (William) (b. 1808, d. 1887) in a paper read before the Royal Society, April 7, 1859. *Vital Statistics*, 1885, 128, 446.
    "Stationary population"—Farr, ib., 475, quoting Herschel.
    Carlisle Table of Milne in *Encyclopaedia Britannica*, 6th ed., *Supplement*, vol. V, 1824, pp. 546 ff., art. "Mortality".
11. That a freed man who had begotten three lawful children became a full citizen. Cf. Malthus, *Essay* I, XIV, of the checks to population among the Romans.
    Halley's suggestion, *Miscell. cur.*, supra 303.

12. Like Leibnitz. See *Dict. de l'économie politique*, art. "De Witt", 868, 1.

Hendriks, *Assurance Magazine*, Journal of the Institute of Actuaries, vol. II, No. VI ff.; vol. III, 93 to 120. Hendriks also reprinted the document for private circulation in a small volume of two parts (I, 1851; II, Supplement, 1852 [1853]).

A copy of the reprint presented by Mr. Hendriks to J. S. Mill is in the London Library, presented to it by Mill in 1866. The reprint might be worthy of a reprinting as giving a romantic incident in the Annals of Life Insurance.

13. The correspondent of the *Assurance Magazine*, William Orchard, in vol. II, 393-4, points out that we have no such records produced and in the same way Dr. Gour (1848) does not give his authority (*Assurance Magazine*, II. 254).

14. Erdmann's *Leibnitz*, Berlin, 1840, p. 190.

Hendriks, *Assur. Mag.*, II. 250, 251. Reprint Part I, 59.

15. Cf. F. Y. Edgeworth's review of Düsing's *Geschlechtsverhältniss der Geburten in Preussen*, 1892. F. Y. Edgeworth's *Papers*, vol. III, 33.

Bernoulli, with one letter i in the name. Hendriks spelt it once with two (—ouilli) in a letter to De Morgan, who answered: "Pray remember the personal interest I take in one-eyed philosophers," he himself being one. See *Palgr. Dict.* (article "Morgan") II. 820 note.

J. M. Keynes, *Treatise on Probability*, 1921, p. 82.

16. Halley and chances—ib., 288, 289, 300.

Farr, *Vital Statistics*, 455.

For Professor Karl Pearson's reinterpretation of Mirza, see Appendix IV.

There is a reference in the *Spectator*, No. 289, January 31, 1711-12 (N.S. 1712), to a "bill of mortality" as an "unanswerable argument for a providence".

V

SÜSSMILCH

DERHAM, CANON WILLIAM
(1657–1735)

The new scientific equipment was beginning to be properly valued at the beginning of the eighteenth century. We are still in England, and within the range of the Royal Society, when we come upon Derham's sixteen Boyle lectures delivered in 1711 and 1712, on "Physico-theology, or a Demonstration of the Being and Attributes of God from His Works of Creation". The lectures became a book (1st edition 1713, 7th, London, 1727). Derham was born in 1657 and died in 1735.

The emphasis is on the last words, "from His works of creation". William Derham, Canon of Windsor, was a devoted naturalist, who thought that the great Robert Boyle, founder of the lectures, being himself eminent in science, would have preferred the lectures on his Foundation to follow his own example and use the observations of physical science as he did, rather than the abstract readings of Richard Bentley, Derham's predecessor in the lectureship. Derham's book included, like Chief Justice Hale's, a vindication of the ways of God to man; but he professed to deal not only (as Hale did) with Mankind, but with the whole World. He left the worlds that are not ours to his later book *Astro-theology*, 1714, adding *Christo-theology* in 1730. In the Boyle lectures our own world plays the chief part. Derham would show design and divine purpose all through creation; and is indignant with the Rev. Thomas Burnet (1635–1715)[1] for finding fault with the Earth. We

136

have already heard that, like Homer, the Earth sometimes nods. Burnet saw more amiss than this, and was displeased with the distribution of Sea and Land. Derham finds all very good. The sea and land balance each other well.

But he deals mainly with animated nature, the divine purpose running through all sentient creation. Considering what the Boyle lectures were required to be,[2] and remembering who Robert Boyle was, what he did for science in the first years of the Royal Society, we must not be prejudiced either in one direction or another by the theological element. Boyle had himself written on Final Causes.[3] His will directed (1691) that the lectures be for the proof of the Christian religion against atheists. Whoever chooses to follow his lectures knows what he has to expect in the view of that limitation. Derham has a real interest in his subject and pursues illustrations in very long footnotes for their own sake. The illustrations may be still profitable here and there for naturalists. His interest for us lies in his evident influence on Süssmilch;[4] he cannot be said to have advanced demography himself directly. "Thou shalt get Kings though thou be none" might be said of him as of Banquo. He is captivated with demography as Hegel long afterwards was delighted with political economy, because it seemed to reclaim for rationality and law a whole region of facts hitherto left outside the reign of both. John Ray, in his *Wisdom of God Manifested in the Works of the*

Creation, 1691, had anticipated Paley in some of his examples of the Design argument, but demography does not figure in his book. It is Derham, not Ray, who served, if any did, as middle term between Graunt and Süssmilch, though Süssmilch says little of Derham and much of Graunt.

In the *Physico-theology* Derham disclaims sympathy with the vulgar error of regarding the whole world as made for man exclusively. In this enlarged view he was anticipating Hutcheson and Bentham, holding, like them, that we must consult the happiness of all sentient creatures. He treats of the air, light, the senses, the bodily members, the food of animals and the room for animals, almost every page laden with illustrations and quotations. He brings us in due time to a chapter headed "Of the place allotted to the several tribes of Animals". "All parts of our terraqueous globe, fit for an animal to live and act in, are sufficiently stocked with proper inhabitants." "Proper" inhabitants are those provided with such bodily organs as can cope with the widely different surroundings and climates. Without this provision of divine wisdom "all the animal world would have been in a confused, inconvenient, and disorderly commixture.[5] One animal would have wanted food, another habitation, and most of them safety. They would have all flocked to one or a few places, taken up their rest in the temperate zones only, and coveted one food, the easiest to be come at and most specious in show; and so would have poisoned, starved, or greatly incommoded one another. But, as the matter is now ordered, the globe is equally bespread, so that no place wanted proper inhabitants, nor any creature is destitute of a proper place and all things necessary to its life, health, and pleasure." "Nay, and as the matter is admirably well ordered yet, considering the world's increase, there would not be sufficient room, food, and other necessaries for all the living creatures without another grant act of the divine wisdom and providence, which is the *Balancing the number of individuals* of each species of creatures in that place appointed thereunto." So he continues in the next chapter, X: "Of the Balance of Animals or the due proportion in which the world is stocked with them." "The whole surface of our globe can afford room and support only to such a number [the balancing number] of all sorts of creatures; and, if by their doubling, trebling, or any other multiplication of their kind, they should increase to double or treble that number, they must starve or devour one another. The keeping therefore the balance even is manifestly a work of the divine wisdom and providence. To which end the great Author of Life hath determined the life of all creatures to such a length and their increase to such a number proportional to their use in the world. The life of some creatures is long and their increase but small and by that means they do not over-stock the world. And the same benefit is effected where the increase is great by the brevity of such creatures' lives, by their great use and the frequent occasions there are of them for food to man or other animals. It is a very remarkable act of the divine providence that useful creatures are produced in great plenty and others [not useful] in less."

"Thus the balance of the animal world is throughout all ages kept even and by a curious harmony and just proportion between the increase of all animals and the length of their lives the world is through all ages well but not over stored; one generation passeth away and another cometh." "The providence of God is remarkable in every species of living creatures, but that especial management of the recruits and decays of mankind, so equally all the world over, deserves our especial observation." When the world was fairly well peopled, there ceased to be need for great longevity, and the common age of man was reduced first to 120 and then to seventy. "By this means, the peopled world is kept at a convenient stay, neither too full nor too empty." If the old longevity had lasted "the world would be too much overrun; or, if the age of man was limited to that of divers other animals, to ten, twenty, or thirty years only, the decays then of mankind would be too fast. But at the middle rate mentioned the balance is nearly even, and life and death keep an equal pace." "It appears from our best accounts of these matters that in our European parts (and I believe the same is throughout the world) that I say there is a certain rate and proportion in the propagation of mankind. Such a number marry; so many are born, such a number die, in proportion to the number of persons in every nation, county, or parish. And as to births, two things are very considerable; one is the proportion of males and females, not in a wide proportion, not an uncertain accidental number at all adventures, but nearly equal. Another thing is that a few more are born than appear to die in any certain place. Which is an admirable provision for the extraordinary emergencies and occasions of the world, to supply unhealthy places, where death outruns life, to make up the ravages of great plagues and diseases and the depredations of war and the seas, and to afford a sufficient number for colonies in the unpeopled parts of the earth. Or, on the other hand, we may say that sometimes those extraordinary expenses of mankind may be, not only a just punishment of the sins of men,[6] but also a wise means to keep the balance of mankind even, as one would be ready to conclude by considering the Asiatic and other the more fertile countries where prodigious multitudes are yearly swept away with great plagues and sometimes war, and yet those countries are so far from being wasted that they remain full of people." "What is all this but admirable and plain management?" the work of one ruling the world.

In proof of those statements Derham quotes freely from Graunt, King, and Davenant as well as from figures furnished by himself from his "own register of Upminster",[7] and contributions from

friends in other parishes. He takes Graunt's authority for a table of the relation of marriages to births
and burials. He thinks Gregory King most likely
to be right in his estimate of the English population—5½ millions and 41,000 marriages; but thinks
Graunt right as to the proportions of the sexes—
14 males born to 13 females. He is evidently comforted by Graunt's inference against polygamy.
That the surplus of males is no work of chance
he thinks has been proved by Dr. John Arbuthnot,
of Kincardine,[8] from the very "Laws of Chance".
John Thomas lays against John "that for eighty-two
years running more males shall be born than
females,[9] and, giving all allowances in the computation to Thomas' side, he makes the odds against
Thomas that it doth not happen so to be near
five millions of millions of millions of millions to
one, but for ages of ages (accòrding to the world's
age) to be near an infinite number to one against
Thomas".

Arbuthnot works out the same argument as
Derham from the balance between the sexes; he
dwells also on the need of a slight preponderance
of the males because of losses in war; and he uses
Graunt's tables and other tables making a series
from 1629–1710. Both had been preceded by Ray.

But Derham's exposition is the most elaborate.
He even drops into an economic argument. It is
good for man to be left to clothe himself because
he can thus adapt himself to all seasons. "In the
next place there are good political [economical]

reasons for man's clothing himself, in-as-much-as his industry is hereby employed in the exercises of his art and ingenuity; his diligence and care are exerted in keeping himself sweet, cleanly, and neat. Many callings and ways of life arise from thence, and, to name no more, the ranks and degrees of men are hereby in some measure rendered visible to others in the several nations of the earth" (219).[10]

His interests, however, are so far from demographical that he quotes Halley's physical papers again and again,[11] and says nothing of the paper on the Bills of Mortality.

If this be deemed "spade-work" we might at least have expected some little help towards the general theory of population and its movements. Derham does indeed cover the ground. But his balance is a pre-established harmony such as Leibnitz had been teaching in his *Theodicée*, 1710 (written circa 1704), and he seems to believe like Leibnitz that this is the best of all possible worlds. The tendency to increase is duly discovered; there is a perpetual endeavour of all animals to multiply; but this presents no such difficulty to Derham as it did later to Robert Wallace; the balance is kept by divine intervention. We are told that certain changes, e.g. the shortening of life, happen; but we do not learn as a matter of secondary causation *how* they happen—by what natural agencies and steps. His language sometimes implies a consciousness that the process is not painless; "prodigious multitudes are yearly swept away with great plagues and sometimes war". We need not share his timidity. As Aristotle says, the gods are not envious; there is no irreverence in trying to lift the veil that hides the secondary causes. But the same fears that led to the notion that a Census was a questioning of the divine government of the world would be roused at the beginning of the eighteenth century by any attempt to frame a general theory of population from secondary causes. On this head Süssmilch is more inspiring.

Of all the "God-intoxicated" men, Derham included, Süssmilch is to some of us the least tedious talker. Yet one might say he tries to intimidate us at the outset by giving to his book a theological title-page, and at first (1741) a title so long that few writers quote more than a small part of it at a time. He had the good sense to reduce it in the second edition, 1761, to the following, adequate for most purposes: *The Divine Order in the Changes of the Human Race shown by its Birth, Death, and Propagation.*

Johann Peter Süssmilch, son of a lawyer in Berlin, was born in that city on September 3, 1707, studied at Halle and Jena, left law for medicine and medicine for theology, is said to have been for a short time a teacher, was certainly doing clerical duty in a country charge for a year. "Da ich vormals als Prediger[12] auf dem Lande gestanden," "Ich habe es in dem einen Jahre meines Aufenthalts in der Land-pfarre erlebt." He found his medical knowledge, such as it was, of some use on that occasion. His political and social surroundings are those of Brandenburg in the time of Frederick the Great, who succeeded in 1740. We may correct our bad impressions, derived from Macaulay's essay, of these surroundings by the first-hand knowledge to be got on Süssmilch's pages. Ordinary life was not very unlike our own of the eighteenth century. Even the spirit of liberty and toleration is not absent from these pages. Protestants, he says, may be better than Catholics, but Catholics are better than pagans. Süssmilch, though living under Frederick the Great, has the courage to remark that Scripture speaks of "men's dominion" over the creatures, but says nothing of a dominion of man over man. He was a democrat, forced by circumstances to be a courtier.

In 1741 he became a *Feldprediger*, "padre", or chaplain in Frederick's army. It was the year of his book's first edition, also of Mollwitz and the invasion of Silesia. From his book, or from his personality, he had evidently impressed higher circles; his titles in his second edition, 1761 and 1762, imply high ecclesiastical promotion, "Königlich-Preuszischer Oberconsistorial-rath, Probst in Köln [an der Spree]". He became a member of the Berlin Academy of Sciences. He gave lectures for the Academy on his own book at the desire of the great Maupertuis, whom Frederick had brought to Berlin. He died of a stroke in 1767.

Süssmilch never quits the pulpit. Even his

high-flown dedication to the King contains a covert sermon on the duties of a king—sure to be taken good-naturedly for Frederick liked his people to say what they thought so long as he did what he chose.

> Hark to the preacher preaching still
> He lifts his voice and plies his sermon.

Yet he is hardly ever tedious, for demography possesses him quite as much as theology. If he is didactic like Derham and has Graunt's unwearied diligence in spade-work, he goes beyond both in trying to bring his results into the whole field of political science and present something like a system of principles in the matter of population. There was nothing like this in the days of Raleigh and Bacon.

In the manner of a preacher he takes a text and comes back to it again and again. It is not "vanity of vanities"; it is not gloomy. But he takes it seriously, and we cannot understand his book without it. If we read Cobbett with pleasure in spite of his vanity we can surely read Süssmilch in spite of his orthodoxy.

The text is from Genesis[13]: "Be fruitful and multiply and replenish the earth and subdue it and *have dominion over the fish of the sea and over the fowl of the air and over every living thing that moveth upon the earth.*" This means what to Süssmilch is of the highest importance—dominion over the creatures. This is the programme set before men;

and their kings and governors are there to help them to carry it out. Man must have no false humility. He has his guide provided for him in his Reason. Men are not ants; they are progressive.

"Reason" in due time, not at first even with Plato and Aristotle and Pliny, led man to discover a "divine order" in the seeming chaos of his own life. Say if you like instead of a divine order Natural Law; and Süssmilch sometimes comes near to that expression: "the laws of the order of Nature" and "the framer of this order of nature" (I. 57, middle). He so interprets his theology as to admit demography, and we need not be perturbed if he so interprets his demography as to admit theology. "The aim of my book is to show there is order in these things; and experience confirms revelation."

He has grasped the principle of large numbers, and leaves us in no doubt from whom he got it. See the preface in vol. I to the "kind and indulgent reader" (p. iii). He is going to "test the rules made, repeated, and confirmed by Graunt, Petty, King, Arbuthnot, Derham, Nieuwentyt, and others", having got some more data than they. No special obligation is confessed to Derham. Petty is judged with some severity; but Graunt is glorified. In the first section of his first volume Süssmilch writes: "This divine order is as elusive as it is impressive. It seems bent on escaping our notice, and the concealment is the easier because there is nothing suggesting to the outward eye any kind of order in births and deaths. Go over our houses one by one. In one you may find all daughters, in another all sons, in others a mixture in no definite proportions. In small groups and villages it is not easy to see any kind of order. The deaths occur by twos or threes in one year, by six or twelve in another year. Who would think there was any rule or order followed?" S'Gravesand's remark in his *Introduction to Philosophy* applies here as to other parts of Physics: "Saepe vero regularitas, quae, consideratis paucis effectibus, nos fugit, ubi plures ad examen vocantur, detegitur." The Church registers are now our great aid in settling those rules. Those Church registers have been kept over centuries (not for demographical, but for ecclesiastical or civic purposes) more carefully after the Reformation than before it. But who before Graunt ever used them to get light on this [divine] Order? The discovery, like that of America, had been always possible, but it required a Columbus to go farther than others in his reflections on old and familiar truths. Thus it fell to Graunt to be the first to perceive an Order in the registers of deaths and diseases in London, and to be thereby guided unto the happy conclusion that there must be a similar Order in other parts of human life. This conclusion stirred up his industry and intelligence[14] to further inquiries by which he has laid the foundations for this science, which not only gives pleasure to its devotees, but stirs us up to know better and reverence more the all-wise framer of this order of

148

nature; which science, too, displays to the gods of the earth set over men as their rulers (the first foundations of Political Science), and teaches them that they can only make themselves and their State happy and powerful by following the rules of that Order which the Supreme Ruler has chosen and established for the populating of the earth."

What is there in Süssmilch that was not in Graunt? The answer is that Süssmilch, writing eighty years after Graunt, has fallen heir to the whole estate of Graunt's spiritual children; he knows all about them and has the "excellent working head" to use what they have given him. The data for England in particular were continually growing, and he uses all he can reach, levying contributions on Davenant, Gregory King, Corbyn Morris, Short, Maitland, always critically. He values Halley, but points out that Breslau was not so simple a sample as Halley had thought, and Halley had only five years against Graunt's thirty. Süssmilch himself had command of statistics for Brandenburg and Germany in general. He drew on Kersseboom and Struyck for Holland, Wargentin for Sweden. There is no appreciation of De Witt, and the subject of Life Annuities,[15] Tontines, and Probabilities is touched very slightly. Euler is thanked for a Table about them. In truth Insurance had already begun to be a special study, a sister study, under the wing of demography, but needing the professional care of the actuary.

Süssmilch is fairly well satisfied with his data for Great Cities, but would like to have much more for the country districts. In the latter he says he has only one parish to help him for deaths at all ages. Here again Euler helped him with calculations.

Like Malthus, he quotes travellers with evident zest—e.g. Chinese travellers (II. 219), Dampier's *Voyages* (I. 203, etc.). He is not only familiar with Deparcieux, but with the anonymous *Intérêts de la France mal entendus*, 1756, calling the author "The Citizen", or "The Patriot". The author is supposed to be le Chevalier Ange Goudar, or Goudard, of Montpellier. Süssmilch has read our *Spectator* in a French translation; but, instead of the Visions of Mirzah, presents us with a simile of his own, coming naturally to the *Feldprediger* after the Silesian campaign.[16] "We enter on the land of the living step by step and without crowding, and in accordance with certain set numbers bearing a certain set proportion to the Army of the living and the Army of the departing. Shortly before entrance there are some as it were ordered out of the ranks; these are the stillborn, and they too have their set proportions. Note too in this emergence from the void into being there come always twenty-one sons to twenty daughters; also that the whole mass of those coming to the light of day is always a little greater than of those returning to dust, and the army of the human race is always growing in set proportions. Now, look at it on the march; it is divided into different squads (*Züge*). Those of the same age make one squad, or you can take them in groups of five or ten years and call these the different squads. They are not of the same size, but there is a definite proportion over the whole army set down for each squad, and the totals have a definite relation to each other. For example, if the whole army amounts to 1,000 millions in life together, the first squad will consist of children from birth to fifth year and amount to a little more than 108 millions; from five to ten to 65 millions; from ten to fifteen, 62 millions; from fifteen to twenty, 60 millions, etc. . . . The children's squad is always the largest. Those that follow are always smaller but in set proportions. Every squad is exposed to particular attacks, and has different ways of falling out. . . . In the first year dies one out of three or four; in the fifth, one out of twenty-five; in the seventh, one out of fifty; in the tenth, one out of hundred; and in the fourteenth and fifteenth, one out of two hundred. The boys have fallen out rather more than the girls, and by the fifteenth to the twentieth year the numbers of boys and girls are equal."

We need not pursue his simile. It is natural for a padre; but it seems less effective than Addison's if we want to produce a vivid impression of the situation on people not already interested in vital statistics. The table used for the simile was a list of deaths in cities which he had drawn up for the year 1756 in a reply to the economist Justi.[17] Justi had taken up a hopeless position, maintaining that the city death-rate was lower than the country's. In his *Manufactures and Factories* he ignores Süssmilch's reply. Justi had thought, by a contrary exaggeration to the Physiocratic, that no country could prosper without manufactures. Süssmilch leans to Physiocracy, but apart from all leanings had no difficulty in showing that the country death-rate was the lower. His Preface (vol. I, page VIII) shows that he was a little annoyed by his opponent's silence. Justi had only mentioned Süssmilch's "book" as "universally known". Strong as he was on finance, Justi was not weighty in vital statistics. He believed a country could never have too many inhabitants, and he was probably thinking of the advantages of concentration as did Petty before him. He said that for brevity's sake and to avoid pedantry he abstained from quoting predecessors (*Polizeiw.*, Pref., 1st edition, last paragraph); but he ought not to have excluded contemporaries who criticized him.

It is an old question among the Utilitarians whether the greatest happiness is of a few intensely happy or of a greater number only moderately so. If Süssmilch had preferred the former he could have quoted "Many are called but few are chosen". He prefers Genesis: "God Himself", he says, "has pronounced in favour of a large population" (*"Gott erklärte sich für die Vielheit und für die Bevölkerung"*).[18] Men need not be massed closely in large cities for this. They are more helpful to each other spread out with a fair and equal division of landholdings. The proportion of country to city was in his day in Europe two-thirds of the whole to one-third, or even three out of four, and this was as it should be, he thinks, and in any case the more men there are the more useful they are to each other. We can say in a wide sense, "It is not good for man to be alone"; and this includes military strength, for defence. In fact, Süssmilch falls into commonplaces as he frankly confesses.

But he extends his view from a narrow nationalism to all humanity. Suppose (he says) we planted a colony of 1,000 Germans on the land once peopled, now desert, at the east of the Black Sea, and left them to provide for themselves, but under orderly rule and with fair distribution of land, if only for the reason of defence (in the manner of Bacon's yeomanry). They would find the need not only for ploughmen, but for doctors and teachers, and even lawyers; they might not need large capitalists; they might be glad to admit foreigners, who would grow up with them into citizens. They would find the need of constant reclamation of wastes and new works and explorations. He asks whether this is after all very different from what has actually happened in Europe. Montesquieu thought we should increase and improve population better if we could break up Europe into many small republics. But Süssmilch says the political constitution and the size of the State matter far less than attention or inattention to a wise supervision of population according to his principles.

Montesquieu and Süssmilch agreed in thinking that population needed direct encouragement. In his well-known chapter, *Essay on Population*, upon "The Checks of Population in the Middle Parts of Europe",[19] Malthus does not spare either of them. He says that Montesquieu in his *Persian Letters* had himself shown the bad effects of direct encouragement of marriage when he pointed to the marriages of youths anxious to escape conscription, but the same Montesquieu writes in the *Spirit of the Laws* that "Europe is still in a state that requires laws which favour the propagation of the human species". As to Süssmilch, Malthus goes on, he has reasoned that marriages will come to a standstill when the food is not capable of further increase, and he has shown that in some countries and parts of countries the number of marriages is exactly measured by the number of deaths. A prince that in a well-peopled country laboured to encourage marriages would be really encouraging deaths, and would be rather the Destroyer than the Father of his people; yet Süssmilch would like such a prince to strive to convert a rate of marriages one to a hundred-and-twenty into a rate one to eighty. Then Süssmilch is inclined towards a general rate or measure of mortality for all countries viewed together. Malthus thinks the measure would be of no use if we got it, but it seems impossible to get it when mortality varies so greatly over Europe—from one in twenty at one place to one in sixty at another. It may be observed that Malthus himself, in devoting a separate chapter to "Checks to Population in the Middle Parts of Europe", instead of describing their condition each by itself as he had done with Norway, Sweden, and Russia, has admitted a closer similarity of economic conditions there than exists among the Northern Nations. Similarity, however, is not identity. We have a fairly fixed point in the difference between the mortality of towns and the mortality of country districts, the former being always the greater. When the proportion of people in the towns to people in the country is, say, as one to three—for every townsman three countrymen—the general mortality may be set down as one to thirty-six; but if the proportion were, say, two to three, the mortality would tend to be greater—say one to thirty-five, or one to thirty-three. So according to Süssmilch the mortality of Prussia was one in thirty-eight, in Pomerania one in thirty-seven to fifty, for the year 1756; so the general mortality for all countries, taking town and country together, would be one in thirty-six. The inquiries of his countryman Wilhelm Crome have thrown doubt on Süssmilch's figures for 1756: Even if the calculation were right the rule would not help us in our time when the towns have so much increased. Another comment of Malthus is that Süssmilch has a tendency to throw years of epidemics out of the reckoning, though he is not alone in this. Malthus even doubts Crome's own figures as drawn from Busching, who had only the data of three years;

Crome has thought that a proportion of townsfolk to country of one to three would imply a mortality generally of one in thirty; for (a) an only moderately peopled State, one in thirty-two; (b) in a thinly peopled Northern State, one to thirty-six (Süssmilch's figure). Malthus thinks that care of health has so far prevailed to improve matters in the cities that an increase of size need not mean an increase of mortality in the old proportion,[20] "even after allowing epidemic years to have their full effect in the calculations". This was at one time a paradox, but now the time gives it truth. He added in the third edition: "The improved habits of cleanliness which appear to have prevailed of late years in most of the towns of Europe have probably in point of salubrity more than counterbalanced their increased size." A long table of Süssmilch on Epidemics is given in a chapter (VI) on "The Effects of Epidemics on Tables of Mortality". His figures for Prussia and Lithuania in 1711, the year succeeding a great plague, as worked out by Malthus, make the marriages one to twenty-six and the births one to ten, showing an increase that would double the population in less than ten years.

In his first essay, 1798, pp. 114–118, Malthus is indebted to Richard Price for those startling figures.[21] The use made of them by the first essay, and the use made of them in their context, by the later essay, differ as a tract from a book. By this time he had got a copy of Süssmilch for himself, and makes a less sensational use of him; still his references in the early part of the mature essay are continual. And he speaks with proper respect of "the valuable tables of mortality which Süssmilch has collected for the periodical though irregular returns of sickly seasons". Malthus himself has been chided by Mr. Talbot Griffith for laying too little stress on diminished mortality, in comparison with increase of births and marriages, as a cause of the growth of population.[22] Süssmilch, like Malthus, mentions both causes, and, perhaps biased by his text, lays no more stress on the mortality than his successor. He recognizes the rising of the standard of living as an element in the problem; it is one reason why Leipzig in his day had fewer marriages than neighbouring towns. But it is not with him what it became to Malthus, a central point.

Effectively there are fifty years between the two; and Malthus, in his vital statistics after his first edition, had the great advantage of a census. Süssmilch, unlike Graunt, does not seem to have felt the want of it at all acutely; what he cries out for is a larger supply of careful registrars of tables. He is fastidious to a fault. We cannot fancy his successor seriously discussing as Süssmilch does whether a diet of fish increases the sensuality of monks, or homesickness (*Heimweh*) the mortality of emigrant Swiss. How could anyone suffer from homesickness in his blessed Berlin? He is evidently uneasy about Switzerland—*warum sie jetzt so entvölkert ist*, contrary to the common notion that since she sends so many soldiers out she must be too full. "It appears", writes Malthus[23] in 1824, "that between 1760 and 1770 an alarm prevailed respecting the continued depopulation of the country." Here again Malthus had the advantage of better information about Switzerland, given in Muret's report of 1766, when Süssmilch was near his end (1767). Many distinguished men have followed Süssmilch in Germany; but he is the Father of German demography as Kersseboom of Dutch and Graunt of English. He was evidently a man of kindly, lovable nature as well as of a solid good sense that seldom failed him and a genuine anxiety to reach the truth. His opinions on theology and politics were not allowed to bias his statistics; but perhaps because so frankly revealed they have obscured the real value of his services by creating the impression that bias was probable.

NOTE TO CHAPTER V

WORKS OF SÜSSMILCH

See Dr. P. Schmidt, in Conrad's *Handbuch der Staatswissenschaften*, 1894, article Süssmilch. Dr. Schmidt was librarian of the Dresden Bureau of Statistics. He gives a full account of the editions, for which see also Dr. Charles E. Stangeland; *Premalthusian Doctrines of Population*, New York, 1904, 213 n.

Mr. Hooper's notice in *Palgrave's Dictionary* is disappointingly brief.

Roscher gives a short but better account in his *History of National Economics in Germany*, I. 421–5 (1874). He counts

Süssmilch himself the Columbus of Statistics rather than Graunt.

For the minor writings, see the list in Dr. Schmidt's article. There was one on children's education, 1745, two on the Epidemic of 1757, one on the Peace with Russia, 1762.

In the Library of the Royal Statistical Society there is the early *Dissertatio de Cohaesione et Attractione Corporum* submitted by "Johannes Petrus Süssmilch, Berolinensis," April 26, 1732, at Jena. S'Gravesand, who is quoted for a celebrated saying in the *Göttliche Ordnung* (see above, p. 148), is frequently cited here. There is also a *Versuch eines Beweises dasz die erste Sprache ihren Ursprung nicht vom Menschen sondern allein vom Schöpfer erhalten habe*,[1] read to the Berlin Academy of Sciences, 1766, but originally drafted twelve years before on the suggestion of Maupertuis, and delayed in completion by the illness of the author. He claims Rousseau on his side (*Inégalité*, Part I, 1750) as against Hobbes, and in some measure against Maupertuis himself and Moses Mendelssohn. This essay on Language is not mentioned by Dr. Schmidt, or Mr. Hendriks (*Palgrave's Dictionary*).

Both books were presented to the Society by Professor Udny Yule in June 1929, who added in 1930 a controversial pamphlet of Süssmilch against J. C. Edelmann, of Berlin, 1748.[2]

Adam Smith's dissertation on the First Formation of Languages did not appear till 1767, when it was printed in the third edition of the *Moral Sentiments*.

---

[1] Essay to prove that the First Language owed its Origin not to Man, but the Creator.

[2] *Statistical Journal*, 1929, Part IV, p. 639; ib., 1930, Part III, pp. 476, 487.

REFERENCES TO CHAPTER V

1. Thomas Burnet was author of *Theologia Sacra Terrae* [see Derham (ed. 1727), 47 n.]. It was the more famous Gilbert Burnet who wrote *History of his own Time*.

2. Compare above, pp. 113, 136.

3. See Kippis (Andrew, F.R.S.) *Biographia Brit.*, vol. II, 2nd ed., 1780, p. 508. Boyle wrote: *A Disquisition into the Final Causes of Natural Things, and whether, if at all, with what Caution a Naturalist should admit Them.* London, 1688.

John Ray. See Leslie Stephen, *English Thought in Eighteenth Century*, I. p. 409.

4. Hull quotes a confession of obligation which is not in all the editions of Süssmilch, but it is safe to depend on his authority.

5. Cf. 252—"a confused huddled state".

The other passages are from ed. 1727, pp. 54, 57, 59, 166, 167, 168 ff. to 177, later 219.

On p. 168 "balancing the number of individuals" is in italics in text. So in edition 1723, chapter IX.

6. The theological writers are not agreed about this. Gibbon quotes Bernoulli as saving that the tail (not the head) of a comet was a sign of the wrath of God. Chapter XLII.

7. Upminster, 174, cf. 22, 23, 51, 67, 79. Graunt *apud* Derham, 174 n. and 175.

8. Arbuthnot's paper for the Royal Society, No. 338; Derham, 176 n., "Of the regularity of the births of both sexes", probably in 1711.

Both writers had been preceded by Ray. Cf. Kippis, vol. I, 2nd ed., 1778, "Arbuthnot", p. 237.

9. Derham, p. 176 n.

10. Cf. Malthus' speculations at the end of the 1st Essay, though the last clause suggests Tolstoy "Que faire?"

11. E.g. 274, variation of the compass. So 25, 32, 35. See above (Graunt).

12. "Preacher"—See *Divine Order*, 2nd ed., 1761, vol. II, p. 459. Cf. II. xxiv. 406, on diseases.

The *Travels of C. P. Moritz*, a Berlin lad, in England, in 1782 (transl. Humphrey Milford, 1924), may be a little too late to show what was the manner of people twenty years before; otherwise it bears out what is said in the text.

Liberty and toleration—Süssm., 2nd ed., I. 556, II. 503, II. 117, § 335.

Dominion over the creatures—ib., I. 41.

Maupertuis—Süssm., 2nd ed., Vorrede, IV.

Frederick—Dedication, cf. text, I. 394.

Hendriks' article on Süssmilch is in *Palgrave's Dict. of Pol. E.*, new ed., III. 502. The date of birth is misprinted 1708 (for the 1707 of the German authorities).

13. Genesis i. 28, quoted in vol. I, Introduction, p. 4, and the repetition after the Deluge, p. 9.

Man and animals—Introd., I. 45, 46, cf. I. 35, 46.

Reason—I. 24, 57.

Divine order and law—II. 347, cf. I. 25, 49, II. 268, etc.

Petty—I. 305, II. 488.

Graunt, I. 56. S'Gravesand, ibidem. The general sense is: "When we look only at a few cases the orderliness escapes us which is revealed when we examine many."

S'Gravesand, author of *Elementa Physicae Mathematica*, has those words in his *Introductio ad Philosophiam*. Süssmilch quotes from him also in the Dissertation *De Cohaesione*, 1732, pp. 23, 38. Nieuwentyt appears there as Cel-nieuwentyt.

14. Wood would have spoken of "his excellent working head". See Graunt, supra.

This science—*Vital Statistics.*

"The populating of the earth"—*Bevölkerung.* Süssmilch, I. 57.

See volume I, p. 1, in the title of the Introduction, and chapter X, XIV, Contents, 50, line 1, 54 middle. It matches *Entvölkerung.* We have the same double usage in publication, invention, etc.

15. Annuities—II. 263, 327, cf. I. 280 (Euler). Cf. Malthus, *Essay*, 6th ed., vol. I, 493. Halley—II. 326.

Travellers—Süssmilch, ib., II. 219, cf. I. 203. *Intérêts de la France*, ib., I. 259, 436, etc. Ascribed now to Goudar. See *Dictionnaire de l'économie politique*, Guillaumin, 1852, vol. I, 834. Hendriks' *History of Insurance*, reprint, 38 n. Arthur Young identifies him with Boulainvilliers (*Pol. Ar.*, p. 297, edition 1774).

16. Simile of the Army—Süssm., ib., I. 52 ff. Table—I. 53 n.

17. J. H. G. von Justi, 1720–1771. See *Manufactures*, 1758, 1761 (*Manufacturen und Fabriken*), cf. Süssm., II. 549. See also Justi, *Polizeiwissenschaft*, 1756, § 151, 3rd ed., Beckmann, 1782, p. 136; ib., § 60, "universally known", p. 55, § 97, cf. § 85.

Avoids quotations from predecessors—*Polizeiw.*, Pref., 1st ed., last paragraph. For country death-rate Süssmilch, I. 79, 80.

The criticism is repeated by Süssmilch in an Appendix to his second volume, 549 ff.

18. Increase and multiply—Süssm., I. 397, cf. 414, 417 ff.,
cf. 398, 400, 404, 405, 406, 411.

Colonization—418 to 420, II. 161.

Small republics—Hume, *Pop. of Anc. Nations*, quarto, 1768,
vol. I, 448.

19. Malthus (later edd.), *Essay*, Book II, chap. V. "Of the checks
to population in the Middle Parts of Europe", 2nd ed., 240, 247 ff.;
6th ed., vol. I. 320, 333.

Süssm., vol. I, §§ 77, 78, pp. 150 ff. Malthus uses the 3rd ed., 1765;
probably the copy got for him by his father in 1799, but not now
at Albury. See *Malthus and his Work* (Unwin), 2nd ed., 1924, 414.

Montesquieu, *Spirit of the Laws*, Book XXIII, chap. XXV.

Crome, 1753–1833. *Palgr. Dict.* (new ed.), 467.

20. Mortality and size of population—Malthus, *Essay*, 2nd ed.,
1803, p. 26. The new paragraph, 3rd ed., 1807, vol. I, 391. So in
6th, I. 335.

Epidemics—2nd ed., Bk. II, chap. VI, p. 253, 254; in 3rd ed.,
1807, chap. X, and so in 6th, vol. I, chap. II; chap. XII, pp. 499 ff.

References to Süssmilch by Malthus—E.g. 6th ed., 278, 296, 321
to 323, 325 to 327, 329 to 335, 404, 477, 487, 493, 499 to 512.

21. Startling figures—2nd ed., 265; 6th, vol. I. 511, 512, only
in substance the same.

"Periodicity" was treated by the late Dr. Soper in an address to
the Statistical Society, December 1928.

22. Griffith, *Population Problems*, 1926, chap. IV, p. 98.

Süssmilch—mortality, vol. I, § 149, p. 276.

Standard of living—vol. I, §§ 133, 134, cf. § 63, p. 134.

Need of registrars—vol. I, Pref. vii, etc., and especially vol. II,
3rd Appendix, 575 ff.

Fish—I. 205, § 98.

Homesickness—II. 539, cf. 537.

23. Malthus, in *Encycl. Brit.*, 1824, vol. VI, p. 320. Cf. *Essay*,
6th ed., Bk. II, chap. V (vol. I), 337.

In *Malthus and his Work*, 1885 and 1924, there is too scanty recognition of Süssmilch; and the views on page 124 (of both editions) would
now be expressed differently.

VI

DAVID HUME
(1711–1776)

The Populousness of Ancient Nations was a subject on which Süssmilch and Hume touched each other. It is the solemn opinion of the learned economist William Roscher,[1] and therefore we must not call it a vulgar error—that the race of man, like the world itself, has an infancy, maturity, old age, and that the modern man together with the modern world is now in old age and decline. We may perhaps be able to say with confidence, *"Antiquitas saeculi juventus mundi"*, but can hardly dogmatize about its middle and end. We can say with Malthus that the American Colonies in his day (1798) were in the bloom of youth, but hardly that the United States of our own day are in their feeble old age. Without accepting this notion, except with Bacon's degree of assent to it, David Hume[2] wrote in 1752 an essay on *The Populousness of Ancient Nations*, contending that there is at least no evidence of a change in man or nature pointing towards a cosmic senility. Men are now what they always were. There are some "extravagancies" to be rejected out of hand. Isaac Vossius (1618–88) had written in 1685 *Variarum Observationum Liber*, in which he gave the City of Imperial Rome a population of 14 millions and the whole of modern Europe in the seventeenth century only thirty, of which he left only two for Great Britain and Ireland.

Vossius had raised the question, but the attention of the learned was diverted from it by a kindred dispute—the battle of the books in St. James' Library, as Swift called it. It was the dispute about the comparative merits of ancient and modern *literature*, and it was started by an essay of Sir William Temple, in itself of no great merit. In the progress of the dispute Richard Bentley had a hard fight to assert his solid learning against prejudice and personalities; but, as he said in words that cling to us, no man was ever written down except by himself; and it was not he who was written down on that occasion.[3]

In the debate on Populousness the issues were more clearly defined, and the matter did not end with Vossius. Richard Cumberland, the philosopher (1632–1718), left a book on the subject published some years after his death: *Origines Gentium Antiquissimae, or Attempts at Discovering the First Planting of Nations* (1742). The debate seems to have simmered on, in the inner circles of the learned. A small seed was then sown that produced a respectably large plant. A *Dissertation on the Numbers of Mankind in Ancient and in Modern Times* was read to the Edinburgh Philosophical Society "several years" before 1753—say 1750—by the Rev. Robert Wallace, Presbyterian Minister in Edinburgh.[4] Hume, who had been abroad as secretary to the English diplomatist and soldier General St. Clair,[5] was back in Scotland and in touch with Edinburgh. It is even said he was secretary of the Philosophical Society in 1752. He may have heard of the *Dissertation* and been unconsciously moved by it to write on the subject himself. On February 19, 1751, he writes to his friend, Gilbert Elliot: "I have amused myself lately with an essay or dissertation on the populousness of antiquity concerning both the public and domestic life of the ancients. Having read over almost all the classics, both Greek and Latin, since I formed that plan— I have extracted what served most to my purpose." He says he has not a Strabo and would be glad if Elliot could get the Advocates' Library to lend him one, were it only a Latin version. But, some months before, viz. April 1750, he had described his work to Clephane as a learned, elaborate discourse, starting some doubts, scruples, and difficulties sufficient to make us suspend our judgment on that head.[6] The affectation,[7] "I have amused myself", was not uncommon amongst authors, and it occurs in Hume's friend, Adam Smith, when in 1764, being abroad with a pupil, he begins *The Wealth of Nations* "to pass away the time". Anyone who reads Hume's essay will see that he told the truth to Clephane; his mind is seriously occupied with the subject, and he realizes that popular prejudice as usual is against him. The topic had been revived effectively by Montesquieu (1689-1755), for Richard Cumberland's *Origines* (supra) were ineffective, and so was the *New Survey of the Globe* by Thomas Templeman,[8] the geographer and antiquarian. Even the paradoxes of so strong a man as Montesquieu could not be ignored, and in his *Persian Letters*, 1721, letter CVIII, he had uttered paradoxes galore, not altogether recanting them in his entirely serious *Spirit of the Laws*, 1748, though toning down what Hume calls his "extravagancies". He had said that the population of the earth is not now a fiftieth of its population in the days of Julius Caesar. In the *Spirit of the Laws*,[9] dealing with the Relation of Laws to number of inhabitants, he tells us: "Italy, Sicily, Asia Minor, Spain, Gaul, Germany were [in pre-Roman days] full of small peoples and swarming with inhabitants; there was no need of laws to increase population. In Roman times decay began, and the Roman marriage legislation came with it. Still, even under Charlemagne [say A.D. 800] there were more people in Europe than now."[10]

Hume had read all this and did not like it. Neither did Süssmilch. When Hume published his essay in 1752 he probably knew nothing of Süssmilch. Süssmilch for his part knew both his Montesquieu and his Hume. He had probably read Hume's essay on *National Characters*, 1748, where Hume criticizes Montesquieu's well-known opinion on the influence of climate on national character. Süssmilch tells us that he himself once thought of writing at large on Hume and Wallace.[11] Not finding time for this, he brings the matter up incidentally in discussion of another question, viz. Has Montesquieu rightly described Christianity as injuring population? He shares Hume's amazement at the statement in the *Persian Letters*. He thinks himself that there were fewer by six or

seven millions in Caesar's time than in his own,
say ten millions against a present sixteen or seventeen. And he is delighted to have "Sir David
Hume on his side": "*Der Herr Ritter Hume ist mit
mir völlig einig*", referring to the essay on Populousness, *Political Discourses*, 1752, "by David Hume,
Esquire".[12] He was not the worse ally for not
knowing our distinctions of title and mistaking
a squire for a knight. His method is very unlike
Hume's. Süssmilch[13] meets the argument that the
cold climate of the North would increase fertility
and furnish the huge hosts of men invading the
South by producing the vital statistics known to
him of North and South; he says there is no difference between Northern men and Southern men in
that particular; there are four children to a marriage
on an average in both North and South. The people
of the North increased because for some time they
had neither plague nor wars, and their increase
made them need to look for food elsewhere than in
their own land. Besides, deportations of conquered
peoples are very common in ancient times, and
they imply that there was supposed to be more
room for them in the places to which they were
deported. So after the Great War of twelve years
ago there was trouble over deportations made by
the Turks; places were found very full. Our own
Dominions are not always eager to have new
immigrants.

Hume for his part makes little or no use of vital
statistics. The chief instance is perhaps[14] "London

at present without increasing needs a yearly recruit from the country of 5,000 people, as is commonly computed". He says: "There were exact bills of mortality kept at Rome, but no ancient author has given us the number of burials except Suetonius [in *Life of Nero*], who tells us that in one season there were 30,000 names carried to the temple of Libitina; but this was during a plague which can afford no certain foundation for any inference."

He agrees with Süssmilch that men are physiologically the same everywhere under any meridian. He appeals to broad general causes since particular facts and figures are so hard to get, the ancient historians being more candid than our own but less accurate. Take the broad general causes. If the ancients had not our smallpox and plague they had slavery, worse wars than ours, and manners unfavourable to the arts of peace and plenty; their agriculture, instead of being before our own, was entirely extensive. If you confront me with figures, I remind you we do not even know the exact numbers of our own people, and the ancients were not more exact but less so [measuring in cobwebs!]. Malthus[15] puts the case neatly: "In the controversy concerning the populousness of ancient and modern, could it be clearly ascertained that the average produce of the countries in question taken altogether [*sic*] is greater than it was in the times of Julius Caesar, the dispute would be at once determined." Hume is equally clear despite his provoking desire to avoid committing himself on

169

any subject whatsoever, and despite his prejudice against great cities like London. He says: "If everything else be equal, it seems natural to expect that wherever there are most happiness and virtue and the wisest institutions there will also be most people."[16] This quotation is from a passage containing thoroughly Malthusian doctrine in the body of it attached to a very un-Malthusian tail: "As there is in all men both male and female a desire and power of generation more active than is ever universally exerted, the restraints which they lie under must proceed from some difficulties in their situation which it belongs to a wise legislature carefully to observe and remove."

If this last clause means direct intervention, it is un-Malthusian. On Foundling Hospitals Hume agrees with Malthus that their drawbacks exceed their advantages. These institutions, and even the convents of modern times, he regards as the modern alternatives for exposure of children, the plan of exposure having the advantage of defeating itself occasionally, parental affection stepping in to save a superfluous child. *Mutatis mutandis*, the last remark might be applied to modern birth control.

If Süssmilch had written his comments he would probably have found the second part of Hume's essay less to his mind than the first. Hume regards small states and small commonwealths as specially favourable to population, and points to Holland and Switzerland as living examples. Süssmilch devotes an appendix to Switzerland as a country exemplifying decline, drawing on a pamphlet by D. Tissot: *Avis sur la santé au peuple*. But his strength lay in his vital statistics of North and South.[17]

Hume[18] in this matter takes up Montesquieu's view as a matter of principle, but finds counteracting causes that made the ancient small states unable to use their advantage, win the wars, the faction fights, the feeble development of trade and manufacture. There was no single city in ancient times whose establishment was set down to the establishment of a manufacture. "A division into small republics will not alone render a nation populous unless attended with the spirit of peace, order, and industry." He would seem, therefore, to decide for the moderns. But he admits all falls short of proof. No trustworthy figures are available. He has an easy task in showing the contradictions of ancient authorities quite apart from the uncertain readings of manuscripts. He finds exaggeration rampant; for example, Greece without Sparta is shown to have been no bigger in the days of their republics than 1,290,000, "no mighty number, nor exceeding what may be found at present in Scotland, a country of nearly the same extent and very indifferently peopled".

A Census for Great Britain (Thos. Potter's bill)[19] was accepted by the Commons and rejected by the Lords in 1753. It was actually to have been an *annual* census, going farther than our own present one; and it had strong support in high quarters. Scotland made one of its own (Alex. Webster's) in 1755, and found its numbers to be 1,265,380 at that time.[20]

Hume goes on: "Choose Dover or Calais for a centre; draw a circle of 200 miles radius: you comprehend London, Paris, the Netherlands, the United Provinces, and some of the best cultivated counties of France and England. It may safely, I think, be affirmed that no spot of ground can be found in antiquity of equal extent, which contained near so many great and populous cities, and was so stocked with riches and inhabitants. To balance in both periods the states which possessed most art, knowledge, civility [we should say culture], and the best police [say civic government], seems the truest method of comparison."

It is a question here of quantity: we are setting the supposedly accurate figures of Hume's day against the confessedly inaccurate figures of ancient writers. To most of us it is a foregone conclusion from what is in a sense an *a priori* argument; it is what Hume calls an argument from *causes* as opposed to an argument from *facts*. This appeal to causes may seem to come strangely from a man who had explained away causation in his philosophy. But this was just about the time (1752) when Hume was renouncing philosophy for history. Let us forget his philosophy on this occasion and we shall probably find the argument convincing and sagacious. Sagacity did not save him from a false prophecy. 700,000 may be the population of London, Paris, and Constantinople: this seems to him a maximum.

"Whether the grandeur of a city be founded on commerce or on empire, there seem to be invincible obstacles which prevent its further progress. The seats of vast monarchies, idleness, dependence, and false ideas of rank and superiority, are improper for commerce. Extensive commerce checks itself by raising the price of all labour and commodities. When a great Court engages the attendance of a numerous nobility possessed of overgrown fortunes, the middling gentry remain in their provincial towns, where they can make a figure on a moderate income. And, if the dominions of a State arrive at an enormous size, there necessarily arise many capitals in the remoter provinces, whither all the inhabitants except a few courtiers repair for education, fortune, and amusement. London, by uniting extensive commerce and middling empire, has perhaps arrived at a greatness which no city will ever be able to exceed." He seems to reckon for a greater London: "Might not one affirm without any great hyperbole that the whole banks of the river from Gravesend to Windsor are one City?"

Six months[21] before his death he wrote to Adam Smith about the American War, which was in its first stages: "Our navigation and general commerce may suffer more than our manufactures. Should London fall as much in its size as I [treated for dropsy] have done it will be the better. It is nothing but a hulk of bad and unclean humours." His biographer, Hill Burton, remarks on this, that London in Hill Burton's own time, 1846, had tripled its numbers since 1776, though the figure 700,000 of Hume was in Hume's time an exaggeration.

Those jesting words about London were among Hume's last. He left the world just as the *Wealth of Nations* was entering it, and he had just time to give the book a cordial welcome. He had helped to put such questions as ours into Economics. He did no more than prepare the way; but it is a great service to prepare the way and make the rough places plainer.

The essay of Hume has been hailed as the best of all his economic writings; which after all are barely a dozen, not to be severely distinguished from the political essays. Hume was not only an economist, but, if we count Cantillon, a Frenchman, the Founder of British Economics. Ricardo, though he too was guilty of detached essays, sits in the seats of the mighty. This particular essay on *The Populousness of Ancient Nations* is on the borderland between Economics and History. The economist is advising the historian on the limits of historical credibility. The essay is usually held to be supremely successful on its own ground. Gibbon was among the early testifiers to its merits,[22] observing that Robertson and Hume have disposed of Mariana and Machiavelli on the superior populousness of ancient nations. "The same extent of ground which at present maintains in easy and plenty a million of husbandmen and artificers was unable to supply 100,000 lazy warriors with the simple necessaries of life."

There was one serious attempt to refute Hume, namely, Dr. Wallace's *Dissertation on the Numbers of Mankind in Ancient and Modern Times, in which the superior populousness of Antiquity is maintained.* With an Appendix containing Additional Observations on the same subject and some remarks on Mr. Hume's *Political Discourse of the Populousness of Ancient Nations*, Edinburgh, 1753. The "Advertisement" or Preface begins: "The author of this Dissertation on the Numbers of Mankind is desired by the Philosophical Society of Edinburgh to acquaint the public that it was composed several years ago and was read before them." He prints it now with the additions that make it a rejoinder to Hume, the date of whose essay is 1752.[23] The Appendix is as large as the original dissertation and turned out to be the more important of the two.[24] Wallace says he will try to discover the "latest fallacy of those pompous arguments which puzzled but did not convince"; and his industry probed all the crevices in Hume's armour, finding no more than a few small ones.

Hume (in his *Autobiography*) says he had made it a rule not to answer critics. He does not break it in the new footnote of the later editions: "An ingenious writer has honoured this discourse with an answer full of politeness, erudition, and good sense. So learned a refutation would have made the author suspect that his reasonings were entirely overthrown, had he not used the precaution from the beginning to keep himself on the sceptical side, and, having the advantage of the ground, he was enabled, though with much inferior forces, to preserve himself from a total defeat." It is amusing to discover, from the footnote inserted in the very first edition of all, that the printing of the *Dissertation* was of Hume's own suggesting.[25] A pleasing commentary on the incident is given in the letter of Marshall Keith to Rousseau (September 1762?): "Je ne me souviens pas si j'ai déjà envoyé une estampe de M. Hume; en voici une. Je vous dirai deux traits de ce philosophe qui m'ont plu particulièrement. Le premier, d'avoir rencontré un nommé Wallace qui écrivait (et bien) contre un de ses essais. David lui demanda quand il serait imprimé. M. Wallace ayant répondu qu'il était alors si occupé qu'il n'avait pas le temps de reviser son ouvrage, David se chargea de ce travail et l'exécuta de bonne foi."

Hume did not go out of his way to quarrel with the clergy. His relations with Wallace were as those of Gibbon with Warburton. Not that Wallace was to be compared to Warburton in powers, and he was no match for Hume even had his case been stronger in itself. But Hume was merciful. The story given by Rousseau in the *Confessions* could hardly have been invented in the case of an ill-natured man. Rousseau projecting a visit to England, the unhappy visit of 1766, writes in 1765[26] that he thinks Hume would suit him as a host, for he is told that Hume corrected the proofs of "Valace's" refutation of him, a magnanimity (he says) like Rousseau's own when he actually pushed the sale of verses written against himself. Rousseau is not a "first-class witness", but there is nothing improbable in the story.

The refutation survives largely because of Hume's connection with it. Wallace noted with satisfaction that it had given birth to a Cambridge Prize Essay in 1756[27]; but he did not pursue the subject farther himself. Having studied the Past in his *Dissertation*, he proceeded to study the Future in a second book (*Various Prospects of Mankind, Nature, and Providence*, 1761, Millar, London). His book includes arguments for freedom and immortality and the goodness of Providence. Each chapter gives a "Prospect". It is mainly the first four that affect us, and they may be read as one general statement. After (I) a general view of the imperfections of human society and of the sources from which they flow, we are (II) presented with the model of a perfect government not for a single nation only (as was Sir Thomas More's), but for the whole earth; then comes a doubt (III) whether government according to the preceding model (involving better equality and better distribution of wealth) ever could have been or ever can be established and maintained in the world. It is a cruel dilemma; he finds that population will grow till the inequality comes back and the suffering comes back. Therefore he concludes (IV) that "the preceding model of government, though consistent with the human passions and appetites, is upon the whole inconsistent with the circumstances of mankind upon the earth", and it was therefore never the intention of Providence that it should be established there. Providence will use man's vices themselves to prevent the establishment of it as not suited to the present circumstances of man on the earth.

Wallace died in 1771, and it was not till 1793 that his difficulty was fairly faced by a like-minded theorist, William Godwin, who was in sympathy with the reforms of Wallace's Utopia and conscious that what objections held against them held against his own. Accordingly, the seventh chapter of the eighth book of Godwin's *Political Justice*, 1793, is entitled "Of the Objection to this System from the Principle of Population", and the objection stated is that of Wallace.[28] The criticism of Godwin by Malthus in the essay of 1798 was thus indirectly a criticism of Wallace. In Wallace's day a vision of equality would appeal to very few; in Godwin's, the period of the French Revolution, to many more. There is no sign that Wallace secured the ear of the public in this second book. But, later, Malthus read it and remembered it.

If Wallace be a visionary, his colleague in the ministry, Alexander Webster, was certainly a "practical man". Instead of looking at the Universe, he defied augury and tried to count the numbers of his own people in Scotland. There was plenty of intellectual activity in Edinburgh, the scene of his activities.[29] Adam Smith had lectured there from 1748 to 1750, and had just gone to be Professor in

Glasgow. Hume, from his country seat at Ninewells, near Berwick, occasionally came up to trouble the waters, and there was much talk of his cousin Home's tragedy of "Douglas" (1754). The Church then embraced a large majority of the people, and was a strong force in public affairs. Webster was leader of the Highflier, or extreme Evangelicals, to which was opposed the Moderate Party—we might call them the Highbrows. He was a leader in debate, and had done the Church some service twelve years before (viz. 1743) in establishing the insurance scheme called the Widows' Fund.[30] Wallace, in this case no visionary, assisted him in the calculations. Webster is described as having "a love of fussiness and of conviviality, in both of which he excelled", being nicknamed from the latter quality "Doctor Magnum Bonum". We must remember that all our descriptions of him come from his opponents.[31]

We have not full particulars of his "Account" from any contemporary record, but it is not hard to imagine the genesis of it. Webster is said to have been called upon by Dundas (afterwards Lord Melville) to furnish for use of the Government a return of "examinable persons"—persons above the age of six and supposed to be fit to undergo public catechizing at the hands of the parish ministers, on the subject of faith and morals. That Dundas was animated by a simple love of statistics is hardly probable, and the cloven hoof appears when we find "Protestants" and "fighting men" among the desiderata.[32]

Webster in good faith applied to the parishes for returns.[33] He could put pressure on the Lowlands from his connection with the Widows' Fund, and on the Highlands and Islands by means of a recently formed Society for the Propagation of Christian Knowledge there, a system of schools subsidized under Royal Charter. He drew up the returns under three heads—Parishes, Shires, Totals. "The author received accounts from a great many ministers in different parts of the country, containing not only the number of souls in their parishes, but their respective ages. From these accounts taken at a medium, and the bills of mortality in Edinburgh, Glasgow, etc., he calculated the sundry ages of the whole inhabitants as stated in the following tables." "Passing over the various uses to which the adjoined table may be applied, it is sufficient for the author's present design to say that it affords a good rule for calculating the number of men able to bear arms throughout Scotland in general and every parish in particular" (p. 77). "488,652 persons in Scotland are under 18 years of age, and 125,899 persons [are] above 56, which together make 614,551. This being subtracted from the grand total 1,265,380, the number of the whole inhabitants, the remainder, viz. 650,829, are the persons between those ages of 18 and 56. At least one half of them may be reckoned males, so that according to this computation Scotland can raise of fighting men more than one fourth of the number of souls which it contains. But, as this proportion includes the blind and lame or otherwise diseased, the author has supposed the fighting men in every parish and shire to be only one fifth part of the number of inhabitants, and these he is of opinion may be reckoned effective men" (4).

The figures for Catholics and Protestants are submitted without comment. The limits of age for the fighting men are, he remarks, those preferred by Dr. Halley to the commoner 16 to 60 (3).

We see that the "enumeration" is full of conjectures, "computations", and assumptions. Yet the author is quite happy about it. He thinks even that his results will make a better basis for the calculation of annuities than those of Graunt or Halley— Graunt's being too bad and Halley's too good. It was a spirited attempt to overcome difficulties then insuperable. We can dispense with the help of the State for many purposes, perhaps more than we ever realize, but, as men now are, we surely need it for a census. The English House of Lords only two years before the *Account*, viz. in 1753, had refused to take a census of England, scared not by military service so much as by taxation. The Bill had passed the Commons. It is possible that Webster as a patriotic Scot was glad to take advantage of Dundas's request, and attempt to score a victory for his country by having the first census, or the first to his knowledge.

In Rae's *Life of Adam Smith* (1895, pp. 399, 400) there are two letters on the subject addressed to an unnamed correspondent, who seems rightly identified by Rae with William Eden. The first, dated December 22, 1785, forwards a Note added to the Survey and extracted from it by Webster's clerk, and in connection therewith mentions that the net revenue from the Customs in Scotland, to his official knowledge, had been increasing rapidly "these four or five years past", and is now more than four times greater than seven years ago. The second letter, dated January 3, 1786, refers to a conversation Adam Smith had had once with Webster just before his death, at a merry dinner party, where (we gather) Webster had been very optimistic about the numbers of the people. The latter adds that in 1779 Webster, making a copy of his Account for Lord North, then Chancellor of the Exchequer, added a Note on the changes since 1755, saying that between 1755 and 1779 the numbers had considerably increased in the great trading centres, but decreased in the Highlands and Islands, as well as in those parts of the Lowlands where farms had been consolidated. Hence he thought over the whole of Scotland the total was much the same.

Adam Smith, in the *Wealth of Nations*,[34] without mentioning Webster, takes a very different view from that author of the number of "fighting men" available. "Among the civilized nations of Europe it is commonly computed that not more than one hundredth part of the inhabitants of any country can be employed as soldiers without ruin to the country which pays the expense of their service."

Webster allowed for one-fifth. As we went far beyond Adam Smith's limit in 1914, we must have been going gradually downwards to our primitive barbarism, or a standard of mere necessaries.

There may have been an indirect allusion of Adam Smith to Webster in that passage. But in the first of the letters to Eden, if Eden it be, there is a very direct reference to Richard Price (1723–1781) as "a factious citizen, a most superficial philosopher, and by no means an able calculator". His offence on this occasion was his gloomy view of the population of Britain; it was going down.

The voice of Richard Price was not the first heard on the subject. In 1757 John Brown, Vicar of Newcastle, the critic of Shaftesbury's *Characteristics*, 1751, had gained an extraordinary popularity for his *Estimate of the Manners and Principles of the Times*. In the review of it in the first number of the *Annual Register* (1758, p. 444), possibly by Edmund Burke, we hear that few books had met with "a warmer reception or severer censure"; it revived the old dispute about ancient and modern times, and the author takes the side of the ancients too narrowly. But the reviewer praises him more than we should praise him now. As the whole book was sombre (Britain's sun had gone down) it does not surprise us to find in it the following passage (186): "The vanity and effeminacy, which this extraordinary pitch of wealth brings on, lessens the desire of marriage; secondly the intemperance and disease, which this period of trade naturally produceth among the lower ranks in great cities, bring on in some degree an impotence of propagation. Thirdly this debility is always attended with a shortness of life both in the parents and the off-spring and therefore a still further diminution of numbers follows on the whole. Matter of fact confirms these reasonings, and lies open to every man's observation. Since the first increase of tillage and home manufactures the increase of inhabitants hath been great in England. Since the vast increase of foreign commerce the increase of numbers is hardly perceivable. Nay there is great reason to believe that upon the whole the nation is less populous than it was fifty years ago, though its trade perhaps is doubled. Some trading towns indeed are better peopled, but others are thinned by the flux of commerce. The Metropolis seems to augment in its dimensions, but it appears by the best calculations that its numbers are diminished. And, as to the villages through England, there is great reason to believe they are in general at a stand, and many of them thinner[35] of inhabitants than in the beginning of this century. It is hard to obtain certainty in this particular without a general examination and comparison. But it appears by the registers of some country parishes which I have looked into that from the year 1550 to 1710 the numbers of inhabitants increased gradually, the two extremes being to each other as 5 to 72, and that from 1710 to the present time the number has been at a stand if not rather diminished" (Section

VIII, 186–9). He goes on to say that gin has lessened the power of our fighting men.

It is agreed among statisticians from Rickman downwards that gin did as a matter of fact retard population at the beginning of the eighteenth century, but the quality of the fighting men cannot have been seriously impaired. The second year after the Estimate was an *annus mirabilis* for military victories in Europe, India, and America.

When the attempt was made after the census of 1801 laboriously to reconstruct the figures for the earlier century, the difficulties were great owing to the badness of registration, but there was convincing evidence of an increasing population. You will find the various conjectural tables in the book of Mr. G. Talbot Griffiths published in 1927 at the Cambridge University Press: *Population Problems of the Age of Malthus*. The results are reached through the returns of baptisms, marriages, and deaths. Though these returns are defective, we cannot do without them. We cannot even now be content with a total every ten years and a blank interval, and we have now since 1837 a better registration than our forefathers ever had.

There is a clear and full account of the defects of our vital statistics, both before and after our first census of 1801, to be found in the March number of the *Edinburgh Review* (vol. XLIX, No. XCVII) for 1829, written when the third census was near at hand and preparations for it were beginning. It is an article on the "Census of the Population", and the writer says (33) he is giving some facts not to be found elsewhere. He is with fair certainty to be identified as John Ramsay MacCulloch, who quotes a page of the article verbatim and without marks of quotation in his *Literature of Political Economy*, 1845, p. 258. The editor of the *Review* till the middle of 1829 was Francis Jeffrey, not succeeded by Macvey Napier till June of that year; and Jeffrey is probably responsible for the last paragraph.[36]

We read in this article (p. 3): "A famous controversy was carried on during the latter part of the American War, between Dr. Price on the one side and Mr. Wales and Mr. Howlett on the other, with respect to the population of England. Dr. Price maintained that the population had gradually decreased from the Revolution down to the period referred to, and that the ratio of decrease had increased during the twenty years ending with 1780."

Richard Price was well known in other fields of inquiry. How did he come to enter this new field at all?

REFERENCES TO CHAPTER VI

1. *Grundlagen der National Oekonomie*, 1879, vol. I, 14, p. 30. Compare Professor Karl Pearson, *Chances of Death*, etc., vol. I, 164. Dean Stanley's youthful Prize Essay, Oxford, 1840, was on the question "Whether States, like individuals, after a certain period of maturity, inevitably tend to decay".

2. Hume, *Essays*, as in quarto ed., 2 vols., 1768, vol. I, 425, 487; Grose's ed., *Essays*, vol. I, 383, 427.
Wallace, *Dissertation*, 1753, p. 34.
Macaulay, *History*, chap. III, 135 (popular ed.).
Compare also Dr. Max Klemme, *Volkswirtschaftliche Anschauungen D. Hume's*, Jena, 1900, p. 77, who holds this essay to be the best of all Hume's economic writings.

3. See Macaulay's essay on Temple, *Edinburgh Review*, October 1838.

4. New North Church. He was also a dean of the Chapel Royal. See Dr. Thomas Somerville's *Life and Times*, 1741 to 1814, Edinburgh. Edm. and Douglas (1861), p. 59. W., he says, "had more originality of mind than any minister in Edinburgh".

5. Hill Burton, *Life of Hume*, I. 235. Elliot was a Selkirk laird; and Hume's property and usual home at this time were at Ninewells, near Berwick.
"Philosophical Society" in 1752, see Rae's *Life of Adam Smith*, 107.

6. "Suspend our judgment", etc., Hill Burton, l.c., I. 297, 298, cf. 326.

7. "Affectation", etc. Adam's Smith letter to Hume in Hill Burton, II. 228. We have found Graunt another culprit (see supra). Compare Ricardo's *Letters to Malthus*, pp. 17, 27.

8. Thomas Templeman. Distrusted by Gibbon, *Decline and Fall*, chap. I, end. For Gibbon's own estimates see chap. II.

9. Book XXIII, chap. XVIII, p. 355, ed. Paris, 1851. Cf. 1st ed. *Lettres Persanes*, CXII, in Collected Works, Amsterdam and Leipzig, vol. V, 286; there is some variation in the latter.

10. Chap. XXIV, p. 365.

11. *Göttliche Ordnung*, 2nd ed., vol. II, p. 579 n.; compare ib., §§ 332 seq., pp. 102–160. Hume, § 344, p. 127.

12. Hume would have answered as he did when a lady facetiously chalked up "St. David's" on his house and David's maid remonstrated: "Many a better man has been made a saint of before", Hill Burton, II. 436. There is a variant of the story in Alex. Carlyle, *Autobiography*, 276.

13. Süssmilch, I. 199, 203; cf. 200 seq. and 300. Compare Hume, *Populousness of Ancient Nations*, p. 424 n.: "We are apt to suppose the Northern Nations more fertile" than Egypt and Africa. Compare 500.

14. Vital statistics, *Populousness of Ancient Nations*, p. 433 ft.; compare 489.

15. Malthus, *Essay*, 1798, p. 55.

16. *Populousness of Ancient Nations*, 427, cf. 444. On large states and small, ib., 446.

17. Süssmilch, II. 537 seq.

18. *Populousness of Ancient Nations*, 466–500.

19. See the *Bluebook Preliminary Abstract of Census*, 1881, p. 1 (Eyre & Spottiswood, 1881).

20. Webster's Survey is in the Register House, Edinburgh, and Mr. J. C. Dunlop, Registrar-General, kindly supplied a copy to the writer.

21. On February 8, 1776. Hill Burton, I. 362; II. 484, 515. Hume died of dropsy on August 25, 1776.

22. Gibbon, 1776, *Decline and Fall*, chap. IX.

23. Rae says (*Life of Adam Smith*, 107) that the Philosophical Society did not meet between the Rebellion of 1745 and the year 1752, in which year Hume himself became secretary of it. If Rae is right, Wallace's "several years" are reduced to "several months".

24. "More important of the two", as happened with Hamilton's edition of Reid, or (to take an instance from Economics) with Böhm Bawerk's *Replies to Critics*.

25. See the careful collation of Grose in his edition of the *Essays Moral and Political*, 2 vols., 1875, vol. I, p. 57 (in the reissue 1898): "If this learned gentleman be prevailed on to publish his dissertation [which Hume had heard him read to the Society(?)] it will serve to give great light", etc.

"Letter of Marshall Keith to Rousseau" [September 1762(?)] in *Rousseau's Correspondance Générale*, ed. Dufour, Paris, Colin, 1927, vol. VIII, p. 97, number 1511. The first part of the letter is quoted in the text. The rest is added as characteristic of the man and the times.

"L'autre est que les lamas étant assemblés en synode pour excommunier cet Antéchrist (car il l'est en Écosse comme vous en Suisse) David se sut asseoir parmi les lamas, et écoutait d'un sangfroid admirable toutes les injures qu'on disait directement contre lui, prenant son tabac et se taisant. Son sangfroid déconcerta les lamas; ils s'en fuirent sans l'excommunier.

"N.B.—Nos lamas ne peuvent qu'excommunier; les vôtres prétendent brûler, ce qui n'est pas une badinerie, pour les brûlés au moins.

"Si vous avez déjà une estampe, envoyez celle-ci à milady Stanhope."

The letter was first printed by Streckeisen-Moulton, *Amis et Ennemis de J. J. R.*, II. 67, 1865. Original in Neuchâtel Library.

26. *Confessions*, Part II, Book XII, p. 560.

Cf. Hill Burton, II. 295.

27. *Prospects*, p. 7.

28. Godwin, *Political Justice*, quarto, 1793, vol. II, 860.

29. See Rae, *Life of Adam Smith*, chap. VIII.

30. *Autobiography of Alexander Carlyle of Inveresk*, ed. Hill Burton (Blackwood), 860, p. 239 seq. His life extended from 1722 to 1805, but the autobiography stops at 1770.

31. Anthony Wood was once pronounced a peculiarly fortunate man, being able to write the lives of twenty of his enemies.

32. It recalls the religious census made by William III and satirized by Swift. See Macaulay, *History*, vol. I, chap. III, 135 (popular ed.).

33. For letters on Webster's "Account" see Rae, *Life of Adam Smith*, chap. XXVIII, 399–401. Adam Smith called Eden's attention to the Account. Letter of December 1785. See later part of this chapter.

34. *Wealth of Nations*, vol. I, 313, MacC.

35. Compare Goldsmith's *Deserted Village*, 1770:

> "To see ten thousand arts combined
> To pamper luxury and thin mankind."

36. See *Malthus and His Work*, 2nd ed. (Unwin), 1924, p. 329 n., on a review by Malthus, so disguised by Jeffrey.

VII

RICHARD PRICE

(1723–1791)

HIS EARLY LIFE AND READING

LIFE IN EAST LONDON

ENTHUSIASMS: UNITED STATES AND FRANCE

FIRST CONTACT WITH VITAL STATISTICS

THE ANNUITY SOCIETIES

THE SINKING FUND. "REVERSIONARY PAYMENTS"

THE PENNY OF THE YEAR ONE

ROBERT HAMILTON'S CRITICISM AND CRUMB OF PRAISE

WILLIAM PITT'S SINKING FUND

DEPOPULATION AND BURDEN OF DEBT

BENJAMIN FRANKLIN

PRICE'S "ESSAY ON THE POPULATION OF ENGLAND"

OTHER AUTHORITIES. THE TWO EDENS

MISGIVINGS

MERITS AND DEFECTS

WILLIAM WALES, HIS "INQUIRY" OF 1781

WITH CAPTAIN COOK AND AT CHRIST'S HOSPITAL

HIS BEST HIT

JOHN HOWLETT'S "EXAMINATION", 1781

PRICE "AN ABLE CALCULATOR"?

ON ROOM, FOOD, AND STANDARD OF LIVING

PREPARING THE WAY FOR MALTHUS

There is a meagre biography[1] of Richard Price, written by his nephew William Morgan (1750–1833), who himself, like so many more famous De Morgans, wrote on finance and annuities, and who was for fifty-five years actuary to the Equitable Insurance Society.

Price, he tells us, was born at Tynton, Glamorganshire, on February 23rd, in the same year as Adam Smith, 1723. He was a son by second marriage of a dissenting minister. At eighteen he was sent to complete his education in an "academy" of East London, and for three years there devoted himself "with ardour and delight" to mathematics, philosophy, and theology. The first of these studies to bear fruit in a book was the philosophy, given forth in 1758 in a small treatise: *Review of the Principal Questions and Difficulties in Morals*, which led to correspondence with David Hume and Benjamin Franklin. Hume was surprised to find so much candour and sense of justice in a clergyman. As Price adds "F.R.S." to his name on the title-page he must have made some contributions to science before that time; and in the closing chapter there is a curious application, to faith and morals, of the doctrine of Chances. We are told that it took him long to overcome the feeling that such secular studies were a waste of time. Yet he was what was then called a "rational dissenter", or Rationalist, and he was a friend of Priestley without full agreement. Broad churchman but devout, he became a preacher first at Newington Green, then at Hackney. He printed theological dissertations and sermons, 1759 and 1767, gaining thereby a doctorship in 1762 at Glasgow, becoming also the friend of Lord Shelburne (later Lansdowne), of Sir William Jones, and of John Howard. One of Howard's last letters, before he caught prison fever and died in the Crimea, was to Richard Price (Moscow, September 22, 1789).[2]

We owe a good deal of his work to the religion that begat philanthropy, and the philanthropy that begat political aspirations. In the second of his two theological books, *Four Dissertations on Providence, Prayer, Reunion after Death, Christianity, and Miracles,* 1767, p. 137 note, under the head of "Providence" he welcomes the idea of Wallace that the world is becoming better; indeed, he looks forward even then to the establishment of truth and liberty and universal peace among the nations. "A scheme of government may be imagined that shall, by annihilating property and reducing mankind to their natural equality, remove most of the causes of contention and wickedness." If only such a Government could be established *anywhere,* it would be imitated *everywhere.*[3]

We must remember that Price was a dissenter in the days when dissenters had real legal grievances; small wonder that they were born reformers. We must remember also that he was destined to have an experience in which William Godwin after him was also to have a share, though a much smaller share. Price was to spend his whole life in East London, the home not so much of the destitute as of the disinherited, who are not so near starvation that they cannot think at all, but who have only leisure enough to comprehend their own poverty and what they lose by it. One great drawback in such a section of a great city is that there seems to be no *genius loci*, and therefore no feeling of home; but there are good heads on the shoulders and the hearts are in the right place.

Small wonder that Price became a visionary, and such as Burke described him in 1790 when Burke wrote *Reflections on the Revolution in France, and on the Proceedings of certain Societies in London relative to that Event*. The "certain societies" were those with which Price was connected; and Burke's famous book begins by a denunciation of a sermon delivered by Price in praise of the French Revolution, November 4, 1789: "A Discourse on the Love of our Country." It was his last public utterance; he died in London on March 19, 1790.

His biographer tells us that curiously as time went on his views of public affairs became gloomier and gloomier while his bodily health and circumstances became better and better.[4] Dyspepsia and home troubles are not the only causes of depression; and we have it on good authority that when the world is changing for the better we feel it bliss to be alive. Price had had that feeling over the rise of the United States, and over the fall of the Bastille. He wrote of the first: "The United States, now the hope and likely soon to become the refuge of mankind." Twenty years afterwards he wrote: "France, to whom once we gave an example, is now an example to us." He had been invited by the Government of the United States to come over and settle there. Such favours did not attract him; and as little did Shelburne's offer to make him private secretary during the Second Rockingham Ministry, 1782.[5] Turgot did not share Price's illusions about America.[6] But this sanguine enthusiasm on Price's part glorifies what is otherwise a somewhat commonplace character.[7] The best of him is that he stirred up others to do their best.

It is into one of the more prosaic scenes, not into the theatre of war and politics, that we must follow him here. We propose to answer the question how Price came to talk of Depopulation.[8]

About 1767 he became interested in vital statistics, not from a purely scientific impulse, but from philanthropy. He was distressed by the failures and misfortunes of annuity societies in East London. He thought he saw their mistakes; he helped them when they would listen to his advice, and finally wrote a book, in which, beginning with them, he passed to larger matters and offered help to the Chancellor of the Exchequer.

So it came about that Price published in 1769 *Observations on Reversionary Payments, on Schemes for providing Annuities, on the Method of calculating the Value of Assurances on Lives, and on the National Debt.*

Morgan, editing the fifth edition in 1792, speaks

in his introduction (p. viii) of the impression made by the first one. "On the first appearance of this work the rage for establishing new societies immediately subsided, a partial reformation took place in some of those which had been already formed, and in a short time the greater part of them, convinced of their mistakes, dissolved themselves. A few indeed persevered in an obstinate adherence to their original plans, but they have lately exhibited a melancholy proof of their own folly, and of the truth and justice of the admonitions which had been wasted upon them."

The book had swelled in its fourth edition into two volumes, with various appendices and a postscript. But even in the original first edition all three subjects of Price, demography, finance, and economics, are given in outline. He begins by pointing out the errors of the insurance schemes; they are the common errors of men who insist on being their own actuaries and proceeding by light of nature. They fixed too low premiums, and disregarded the difference made by age and by sex.[9] Of all the societies under review the least laudable was one calling itself the Laudable Society.[10] Against all such he holds up Dr. Webster's Widows' Fund for the Scotch Ministers as a shining example of right principles successfully carried out. This is the same Dr. Webster who drew up the *Account of the Population of Scotland*, 1755, and he had laid the foundations of this insurance system in 1748. The Middlesex clergy (the Dissenter Price is probably not unwilling to note) have by no means reaped the same success, nor deserved it. Price, you see, is not merely critical; and it should be added that he traced out a national Savings Scheme for the "lower part of mankind", out of weekly contributions, giving them something better than the hateful Poor Law Relief.

He allows that in taking us over from Widows' Funds to the National Debt and Sinking Fund he is jumping away from his main subject, and here is his apology: "The National Debt is a subject in which the public is deeply interested. Some observations have occurred to me upon it which I think important; and for this reason, though foreign to my chief purpose in this work, I shall beg leave to offer them to public attention."[11] The main subject was the Widows. The Debt and the Population come in as episodes, but they come in from the first in 1769.

A common feature of the Widows' Fund and the Debt is the idea of procuring tranquillity and confidence by judicious provision for the future. The humble individual and the large nation have both a future to provide for. In the year 1769, the sixth year of peace after the Seven Years War, in which Süssmilch was "padre", both matters were in agitation. The peace had given Englishmen·time to realize the enormous growth of the National Debt, from 16 millions in 1700 to 146 millions in 1763, then dropping only to 138, or 136 when war began again in 1776.[12] To borrow at interest (he reminds us) means returning, for a sum lent to you, an indefinitely greater sum; and this is just what we go on doing. Even terminable annuities would help;[13] but the more excellent way is that of a Sinking Fund, of which he submits a revised version. There had been Sinking Funds before, and there was an anonymous *Essay on the Public Debts of this Kingdom* (1726), which brought them in, and to which he confessed obligation. If statesmen in office had only left the old Sinking Funds intact we should by this time be saved and happy by the magical effect of compound interest. "Money in a sinking fund if never alienated is improved at compound interest, but when procured by a loan bears only simple interest." "One penny put out at our Saviour's birth to 5 per cent. compound interest would in the year 1791 have increased to a greater sum than would be contained in 300 millions of earths all solid gold. But if put out to simple interest it would in the same time have amounted to no more than seven shillings and sixpence. All Governments that alienate funds destined for reimbursement choose to improve money in the last rather than the first of these ways."[14] He speaks as if interest grew of itself unconditionally at all periods and places. Such passages as this led Adolf[15] Held to remark on Price's "lack of historical sense". Dr. Robert Hamilton (1743–1829), who wrote on the National Debt in 1813, is free from rhapsodies himself, but is careful to be just to Price. Think, he says, of "the effects which his plan has produced upon our system of national finance. It has not shared the common fate of the projects of private individuals and vanished in neglect and oblivion. It is the basis of Mr. Pitt's Sinking Fund,[16] adopted fifteen years after its first publication and now followed out for twenty-seven years, and, although with some deviations, yet on the whole with a steadiness seldom experienced in public measures for so great a length of time, and under a succession of different administrations." Ricardo[17] thinks that a Sinking Fund, honestly applied, is favourable to the accumulation of wealth. The difficulty is that the honest application lasts only a short while, immediate reduction of taxes being more popular than ultimate redemption of debt.

Price himself was not satisfied with the Government's handling of the matter. The Debt in England had not the momentous consequences which it had in France, where it produced the Revolution; but it was a cause of anxiety to Price for the rest of his life, not the less because of the fear of a fresh start. Price even pressed the importance of a Sinking Fund on his friends in America, to little purpose.[18]

It was not by accident that the question of population, the growth or the decrease of it in Britain, came up alongside this question of finance. The idea expressed long afterwards by the opponents of the Corn Laws that our huge Debt (three times the figure of 1786) will break us down unless we have a larger population to support it was probably present in Price's mind,[19] though it seldom comes to the surface so emphatically as with those agitators. Listen to this, for example, from Perronet Thompson's *Abridgement of the Catechism on the Corn Laws* (1839), p. 13: "One way Providence has left open to us, and that is to outgrow the evil. Allow the wealth and ability of the nation to double themselves by removing the Corn Laws and the debt which is now overwhelming will be comparatively insignificant—in the same way that the load which buries a vessel of one hundred tons will be only comfortable ballast for one of two hundred."

Perhaps Price was more anxious to emphasize danger than to palliate it by suggesting the alternative remedy: "Instead of reducing your debt increase your numbers." Though he stands by the old-fashioned view that "the strength of a state consists in the number of its people", he might well have thought it best to shake the burden off first and increase population afterwards.[20]

The words just quoted (about the strength of a State) occur in an essay appended to the *Observations* and printed in the Transactions of the Royal Society, after having been read to it on April 27, 1769, the year of the first edition of the book. The essay had taken the form of a "Letter to Benjamin Franklin on the Expectations of Lives, the Increase of Mankind, the Number of Inhabitants in London, and the Influence of Great Towns on Health and Population". Price was F.R.S. himself, but seems to have doubted whether the Royal Society would accept such a paper without special recommendation, which, of course, Franklin gave. Franklin's own *Observations*[21] *concerning the Increase of Mankind* made a wide impression everywhere. He made much of the contrast between the ample room of the American Colonies and the narrow limits of England. Malthus learned much from Franklin, and Franklin's principles would hardly support Price's conclusions. He may have helped Price with the Royal Society in the same generous spirit in which Hume encouraged the publication of Wallace's *Dissertation.*

The subject was probably agitating Price's mind because of his Insurance Societies; his attention was naturally drawn in the first instance to the "births, marriages, and deaths" of London. He thought even London was declining, still more the rest of England, since the Revolution of 1688.

The *Observations* of Price are not well arranged. Part follows part, appendix appendix, as the editions grow, with additional essays and an additional postscript, the postscript being, as in old-fashioned private letters, perhaps of chief importance.

There is, however, a fairly complete clear statement of Price's views on this subject, detached from the other two. It is in a separate pamphlet printed by him in 1780: *An Essay on the Population of England from the Revolution to the Present Time with an Appendix containing Remarks on the Account of the Population, Trade, and Resources of the Kingdom in*

Mr. Eden's Letters to Lord Carlisle. It was this essay more especially that drew the fire of his chief critics.

The Eden of the title is not Frederick Morton Eden (1766–1809), author of the great book on the *State of the Poor* (1797, 3 vols., quarto), a history of the labouring classes from the Conquest downwards, but William Eden (1744–1814), secretary to the Earl of Carlisle, and afterwards himself a peer, Lord Auckland. Of a series of *Letters* (printed as a pamphlet) to his patron, dealing more with politics than demography, he devoted the fifth, issued in 1780, to a rather halting refutation of Richard Price, pointing out reasons for a suspense of judgment, but inclining towards the opposite view to Price's. He is not quite sure that a census which would decide the matter is practicable for such a nation as we are. If Adam Smith's biographer is right in identifying Eden with that economist's correspondent on the subject of Price and population, 1785–1786,[22] he drew from Adam Smith a decided answer that would nerve him for a fresh effort in the latter year. As he speaks in his third letter to Carlisle (88) of "our friend, Mr. Adam Smith", Rae is probably justified.

Here is the general course of Price's argument in 1780:

He thinks that for London the bills of mortality show the decrease, and they are more accurate now than in Graunt's time because there are fewer Dissenters. Davenant at the end of the seventeenth century gives the number of the houses in England at the Revolution as 1,319,215, which multiplied by six as the supposed number of each household gives 7,915,290 as the population. Price finds the number of houses in 1780 to be under a million, and the population therefore under six millions—no more than in Naples. On this it was remarked that the reckoning before the Revolution was by the Hearth Tax, with all its exemptions and evasions, and after the Revolution it was by the Window Tax with peculiarities of its own, an equally bad foundation. Then it was said that Davenant in his estimate meant families, not houses, and the multiplier for each house was too high; it should be rather five or four and a half than six.

Another of Price's proofs was the dwindling of the excise, especially on strong liquors. It was remarked then that between 1740 and 1750 gin was almost free, and the excise regained its force thereafter.

A better line of proof was the appeal of Price to the facts of house-building. There was admittedly an increase of the better class of houses, especially in London. Price thought this obviously meant a decline in the numbers of those who live in the worse class of houses. He may have meant that the rich are becoming richer and the poor poorer. Price allows that there has been a general increase in the population of towns over England generally, and he can only say that it meant depopulation elsewhere—elsewhere meaning the rural districts, towns being worse for population than plagues,

famines, or wars—or else it meant increase merely
of trade, which he seems to think employed fewer
hands. But his economic positions are sometimes
shifted.[23] "Luxury has lost to us 200,000 of our
common people in eighteen years." "The causes of
depopulation have prevailed so much as to render
it an evil which could not but happen,—the
increase of our navy and army and the constant
supply of men necessary to keep them up, a devouring capital, too large for the body that supports it,
the three long and destructive continental wars in
which we have been involved, the migrations to
our settlements abroad, and particularly to the
East and West Indies, the engrossing of farms, the
high price of provisions, but above all the increase
of luxury and of our public taxes and debts."

Besides those causes he mentions paper currency,
and the tribute we pay to the foreigners as interest
on what they have taken of our National Debt. All
the worse because at this time, 1780, we have not
a friend in the world. To some economists the
following is worse heresy—that our trade, which is
called so flourishing, is simply carrying away our
treasure and impoverishing us to pay the foreigner.

In the matter of emigration he had forgotten
what he himself wrote in 1776 in reply to Josiah
Tucker: "Unless the Kingdom is made a prison
to its inhabitants, these migrations cannot be
prevented, nor do I think they have any great
tendency to produce depopulation. When a number
of people quit a country there is more employment

and greater plenty of the means of subsistence left for those who remain; and the vacancy is soon filled up."[24] This argument was put even better in an anonymous book, which may be Edmund Burke's: *An Account of the European Settlements in America*. "The barbarism of our ancestors could not comprehend how a nation could grow more populous by sending out part of its people. We have lived to see this paradox made out by experience, but we have not sufficiently profited of this experience, since we begin, some of us at least, to think that there is a danger of dispeopling ourselves by encouraging new colonies or increasing the old. If our Colonies find, as hitherto they have constantly done, employment for a great number of hands, there is no danger but that hands will be found for the employment. That a rich trading and manufacturing nation should be long in want of people is a most absurd supposition, for, besides that the people within themselves multiply the most where the means of subsistence are most certain, it is as natural for people to flock into a busy and wealthy country that by any accident may be thin of people as it is for the dense air to rush into those parts where it is rarefied."

Mutatis mutandis we can apply this reasoning to the case of the migration from country into town, which is going on now, in the twentieth century, without ceasing. Though the dense air does not rush in to fill the gaps in the country, it is not because the total population is lessened, but because the forms of industry have changed and the numbers go where the need for them is greatest. At least this is the tendency where industrial motives to draw men into the country are the prevailing motives. Price himself, speaking like Graunt of an overgrown capital, curiously attributes to London itself a declining population, not observing that this implied that the "devouring" influence was *pro tanto* diminished.

There is an interesting passage introduced in the third edition of Malthus' *Essay on Population*, and included in all subsequent editions: "An estimate of the population or mortality of London before the late enumeration always depended much on conjecture and opinion on account of the great acknowledged deficiencies in the registers; but this was not the case in the same degree with the other towns [Norwich, Northampton, Newbury, Manchester, Liverpool] here named. Dr. Price, in allusion to a diminishing population, on which subject it appears that he has so widely erred, says very candidly that perhaps he may have been insensibly influenced to maintain an opinion once advanced." The exact words of Price are: "Upon the whole" (a favourite phrase of his), "I beg it may be remembered that my opinion in this instance is by no means a clear and decided conviction. I may probably be influenced too much by a desire to maintain an assertion once delivered. Some time or other perhaps the Legislature will think this a point worth attention."[25] And there are other expressions of the sort: he was "open to receive any evidence". "I know I may possibly be under the influence of those undue biases to which Mr. Eden ascribes the apprehensions which many now entertain of the public danger."

The comment of Malthus gives a wrong impression. Price did not live to see the Census, and could not have guessed how widely he had erred. He would have been astonished could he have foreseen that in his own despite he had led Malthus to find a danger where he himself looked for a blessing. He had already had this very experience when Edmund Burke wrote the *Reflections on the French Revolution*.

To the politicians he left the legacy of an inviolable Sinking Fund, to the actuaries he left the Northampton Life Table, which they find a delusion and a snare. He left nothing perfect, but his very mistakes have helped us towards perfection.

His own theory of human life savours of the idyllic. If all men were good there would be no problem. Each man would live out his full length of days, and we should pass from the world in painless sleep. Wallace might have shown him the other side of the matter, and it was this idyllic passage that seems to have brought Malthus' critical revolt to a head.

There were others in revolt before him. If Price was himself an indifferent reasoner, whether in demography or in economics, he was the cause of good reasoning in other men. There are two specially good answers to him on Depopulation. The first [26] is from the pen of William Wales, F.R.S., Master of the Royal Mathematical School in Christ's Hospital, who had been with Captain Cook in the *Resolution* (on his second voyage round the world, 1772–1775) as Astronomer. Wales deals more particularly with the increase since 1750, by means of Questions addressed to old inhabitants concerning houses and cottages, being "mobbed" for his inquisitiveness in the North Riding of Yorkshire.

He also applied to the subject his own knowledge of London, and even his experience in the Blue-coat School. He thinks there is a distinct change for the better in the matter of air, and cleanliness, in London, leading to a reduction of the death-rate there. "Nothing, I am convinced from much experience," he says, "contributes so much to health as cleanliness, and I am persuaded that in the *Resolution* we owed more to Captain Cook's care in this respect than to every other cause put together [*sic*]." Cook, it is generally admitted, had made a new beginning as far as sailors were concerned by the air and cleanliness and the choice of diet, for avoidance of scurvy—so that the *Resolution* came home, having in three years in this second voyage lost only four men and only one by sickness out of 118, while the experience of the sister ship was far otherwise, and in Cook's first voyage he had lost thirty men out of eighty-five. It might have been a good example for Mill's *Logic* to illustrate the method of Agreement and Difference. Cook in the matter of rules of health may have been anticipated by Moses, and by Bacon in the *Atlantis*; but as far as English seamen were concerned he well deserved what he received from the Royal Society in February 1776, *in absentiâ*,—the Copley gold medal, membership of the Society, and a laudation by Sir John Pringle.[27]

William Wales, though proud of his Captain, rightly regards that Captain's successful experiment as a symptom of the times, an instance of a general tendency. When Brown of the *Estimate* thought our standard of life was falling it was really rising, and the conditions of life in London more especially were being improved, all through the period since the Revolution, when degeneracy was supposed by Brown and his like to be rampant. Attention to the rules of health seems to have gone hand in hand with attention to the vital statistics. Wales gives figures to show that better buildings, better air, greater cleanliness, better water supply, lessened mortality. It is delightful to read too that "providence has cast my lot in an age which is as desirable as any that have preceded it for many generations". Then follows one of the few observations of Mr. Wales that are still generally quoted by statisticians: "There is one cause why the number of births may be higher now than formerly without supposing a greater number of people to produce them, although as far as I know it has never been adverted to before, and which with all due submission to the opinions of medical people is this: Will not every cause which produces a greater degree of mortality impair the bodily faculties of the living before it produces death, and amongst others the procreative faculties also? If it will, and there were some cause which produced a greater degree of mortality formerly in the City of London than now, as the following tables seem fully to show, that cause would operate to produce fewer children formerly than are produced now when that cause appears not to operate so strongly in producing absolute mortality as it has done before."[28]

The essay of William Wales was followed in the same year, 1781, by a still better *Examination of Dr. Price's Essay on the Population of England and Wales, and the Doctrine of an Increased Population established by Facts.* The author was the Rev. John Howlett, Vicar of Dunmow, Essex. He begins by a compliment to Wales and a reference to Goldsmith, and then deals with the repeated assurances of "an able calculator, the Rev. Dr. Price". You may remember that this phrase occurs in the letter of Adam Smith, 1785 (supra), where it is evidently a reminiscence of Howlett. Howlett may have agreed with Adam Smith, but felt bound to salute his opponent before the assault.

Howlett covered the ground so much more thoroughly than Wales or Eden that his book was generally received as conclusive. His conclusion is that the population has increased by one-third since the Revolution, about one-sixth between 1760 and 1780, and is now between 8 and 9 millions.[29] Instead of following his figures we may look at some of his general observations, and judge how far there was any convergence towards the theories usually called Malthusian.

If we take the three elements in the problem of room, food, and standard of living, and if we give a wide interpretation to each, we can extract a commentary on them out of Howlett. "If proper attention were always paid to choice of situation, to public, domestic, and personal cleanliness, to the introduction and circulation of fresh air and some other circumstances, I am inclined to believe that the largest cities, notwithstanding the many disadvantages inseparable from them, might be rendered nearly, if not altogether, as healthy as the healthiest of country parishes." In the broader sense of "room", room in the settlements abroad has the same effect on our farmers as the prospect of employment, support, and maintenance from our towns here; so "a numerous offspring is the consequence; this is a powerful incitement to the most active industry". "Those provinces in Spain which send the greatest numbers to their South American colonies still remain the fullest of people."

In the matter of food, he says, it is unsafe to make a particular staple article of food a measure of numbers till we know whether it has remained the article of universal consumption. Howlett has gathered from a correspondent in the North of England the information that people there now consume at least ten times as much beef and wheaten bread as their forefathers did in 1688. He adds that in spite of Richard Price he will not call this the growth of mere luxury: "I can only view it as a pleasing evidence of the increase of industry, the improvements in agriculture, and the blessings of heaven which seldom fail to attend them." This change need not show an increase of numbers. We should say it would show an increase of efficiency, which is the modern criterion of the goodness of food. In this case the *degeneracy, at least,* of the English people would have a presumption against it.

Howlett does not put it quite in this way, but he is perfectly aware that the higher standard of living will tell against marriage. "The marriages among the lower classes of Society are to those of the middle and higher orders [observe the old-fashioned mode of speech] in the proportion of nearly nine to one.[30] These latter have a certain pride of station, a shame and fear of descending beneath it, a superior perhaps a false refinement of thought, a luxury and delicacy of habit, a tenderness of body and mind, which, rendering formidable the prospect of poverty and thereby checking the impulses of nature, frequently prevent matrimonial connections. The former, on the contrary, having none of these impediments to surmount, readily obey the suggestions of natural constitution, and embrace the first opportunity of an inseparable union with someone of the other sex. . . . Let the worst happen that may, it will be nothing more than what they have been enured to in their earlier years." Dr. Johnson, in an entertaining dialogue in 1769 with Boswell, says the same: "A man is poor, he thinks: I cannot be worse off and so I'll e'en take Peggy."[31] Such reflections of the laity prepare the way for the Malthusian doubt whether increase is always desirable. The doubt crossed few minds in the middle of the century and the next twenty years. You remember Goldsmith's jocose beginning of the *Vicar of Wakefield*:[32] "I was ever of opinion that the honest man who marrried and brought up a large family did more service than he who continued single and only talked of population." It shows how the wind was blowing. It was, however, a long way from a clear idea of *a persistent force resisting depopulation*, such as impressed Malthus, at the end of the century. Others knew of its effects in particular cases, but it seemed to Malthus that nobody but himself in 1798 was quite aware of the enormous power of it. And since at first he seemed to himself to stand alone, he exaggerated his points of difference from ordinary views.

Others were really moving in his direction without generalizing the explanation of observed facts. Howlett had done this in regard to the engrossing of farms, the substitution of one large for many small, which at that time frequently followed the enclosure of commons and stood on its defence along with that enclosure.

If it be true, Howlett says, that engrossing of farms and enclosure of commons increase the poor and the parish poor rates, this at any rate means increase of population. He shows from Arthur Young's writings that enclosure has increased the food. In 1786 Howlett wrote a tract reaffirming these positions. It shocks us perhaps to find him seeing only the bright side. Arthur Young had set the example.

REFERENCES TO CHAPTER VII

1. For its defects, see *Edinburgh Review*, June 1815, p. 171 seq. For Price on Morals see *Life*, pp. 15, 18, 23; for his scientific attainments, ib., 24, 25, 38, cf. 453 and 33, 34. The works of Price were published by Morgan in 10 vols., 1816.

Compare the volume on *Moral Sense*, dealing with the philosophers who explained morality thereby, in *Library of Philosophy* (Allen & Unwin), 1930, pp. 117 seqq.

2. See Baldwin Brown's *Life of John Howard*, 1818 (quarto), pp. 440, 615. *Life of Price*, 141.

3. Compare Josiah Tucker's prophecy in Leslie Stephen's *English Thought in Eighteenth Century*, II. 303: "In half a century [from 1774] two great and right measures will have been adopted—a separation from America and a Union with Ireland."

4. France and U.S. See *Life*, p. 80, cf. 76, and *Love of our Country*, Appendix, p. 36 of 6th ed., 1790. Health better and better, etc., *Life*, 46, 47.

5. *Life of Price*, 99. Lippert in *Handwörterbuch* thinks that the offer was accepted, and he proceeds to draw inferences therefrom, of doubtful force.

6. Turgot in Price's *Life*, 74, circa 1780.

7. Not otherwise in Mrs. Chapone's eulogy of him as "Simplicius" in her *Miscellanies*, Essay I, quoted in Price's *Life*, 184, 185.

8. Fowler in his art. "Price" (Richard), *Dict. of Nat. Biogr.*, forgets to mention this controversy, caring more about Price's ethics, which followed Cudworth and Wollaston's "intellectual system". See *Moral Sense*, 1930, pp. 117 seqq.

9. Not that the critic himself avoided all those traps. See, e.g., Farr's *Vital Statistics*, p. 469.

10. "Laudable Society", Price, *Revers. P.*, 5th ed., vol. I, XVII, XVIII, cf. 109.

On Webster, ib., I. 91, cf. 117; Middlesex, ib., I. sect. II. 86 ff. Weekly contributions, I. 140 n., cf. XXXI.

11. Beginning of chapter III, "Of Public Credit and the National Debt", 5th ed., I. 181. In the third, page 133, he says: "I cannot help here begging leave to offer observations" that have occurred to him.

12. Price, 5th ed., I. 182. Robert Hamilton, *Inquiry into the National Debt*, p. 69, says that the funded debt in 1786 was £238,231, 248, 2nd ed., 1814.

13. Terminable annuities *versus* Sinking Fund, 5th ed., I. 183,

185, cf. 217, 225. The anonymous Essay, 1726. See Price, 5th ed., I. 208. The essay is attributed to Nathaniel Gould, M.P., director of the Bank of England. See MacCulloch, *Literature of Polit. Econ.*, pp. 320, 321.

14. The penny of the year One, ib., 225, 226.

15. Adolf Held, *Sociale Geschichte Englands*, 1881, vol. I, 72, "Mangels an historischem Sinn".

16. Pitt. See *Life of Price*, pp. 122 ff. Price says that, out of three suggestions submitted by him in 1786, Pitt adopted the least good (124). Compare Hamilton, 2nd ed., 1814, p. 134.

17. Ricardo. See *Encycl. Brit.*, 6th ed., art. "Funding System" (1820); *Works*, ed. MacCulloch, pp. 537, 538.

18. Friends in U.S.—*Life of Price*, 105, 106.

19. Present in Price's mind—see, e.g., 5th ed., I. 104, 204, 274; II. 227. *Essay* of 1780, p. 31: "That load of debts which has pressed so heavily on our population is increasing faster than ever."

20. Strength in numbers—5th ed., vol. I, 274.

21. Franklin's *Observations*, Philadelphia, 1751. Arthur Young writes of it (*Political Arithmetic*, 1774, p. 68) as "Said to be by Dr. Franklin, where more good sense upon these subjects will be found mixed with a few thoughts not equally striking than in half a score of complaining volumes".

22. Rae, 398 to 400.

23. E.g., *Essay*, 28, contradicting 27, cf. 29.

Too large for the body. Compare supra, Petty and Graunt.

Paper currency, Price, *Essay*, 69, 70; tribute to foreigners, 67, 68. So he thinks it a sign of Scotland's poverty that it has so little gold coin. *Essay* of 1780, p. 17 n.

24. *Civil Liberty, the Principles of Government and the Justice and Policy of the War with America*, 3rd ed., 1776, p. 101 n.

European Settlements, 2 vols., small octavo, 1st ed., 1757, 2nd, 1758. The quotation is from the 2nd, vol. II, 293, 294.

25. Malthus, *Essay*, 3rd ed., 1806, vol. I, 461, and later ed., e.g. 6th, 1826, vol. I, 407.

For the concession of Price, see Postscript, 1783, 4th ed., repeated in 5th, 1792 (checked by Morgan from author's MSS.), vol. II, 346. Compare Preface to 4th ed., 1783, and *Essay* of 1780, Pref. IV. The description of normal longevity ending in painless sleep is from ed. 1792, vol. I, 370, II, 265. The printer has put 243 for the latter figure, and Malthus reproduces the mistake in his citation.

26. William Wales, *An Inquiry into the Present State of Population in England and Wales and the proportion which the present number of inhabitants bears to the number of former periods*, by William Wales, F.R.S., and

Master of the Royal Mathematical School in Christ's Hospital. London, 1781, 8vo, pp. 79. See E. D. Rogers, in *Palgrave's Dict. of Polit. Econ.*, art. "Wales". The book is reviewed in the *Annual Register* of 1780 (210). Wales gives his questionaire, pp. 6, 7. The mobbing, p. 7. Providence, etc., 21.

27. Best account in Dr. Andrew Kippis' *Biographia Britannica*, 1789, vol. IV, pp. 189, 190. Compare Farr, *Vital Statistics*, 493; Professor Laughton in *Dict. of Nat. Biogr.*, art. "Cook".

28. Graunt in Hull's *Petty*, II, 368: "The more sickly the years are the less fecund or fruitful of children they also be."

29. See, e.g., *Annual Register*, 1781 (230), where Howlett is said to have "much the appearance of being decisive", but a tract on *The Uncertainty of the Present Population of the Kingdom* has driven the reviewer back into "doubt and difficulty". He expects light from a new edition of Price's *Observations*, but has no illumination of his own to give us.

30. On page 28 a note confesses a little exaggeration, and suggests the proportion of 6 to 1.

31. Compare Malthus, *Essay*, IV, ii (6th ed., 1826, vol. II, 281), end of chapter: Of the effects on society of moral restraint. "Let what will come, we cannot be worse off than we are now."

32. *Vicar of Wakefield*, 1766; *Deserted Village* (dealing directly with depopulation), 1770.

VIII

ARTHUR YOUNG
(1741–1820)

Arthur Young's studies and writings and travels over a long life (1741-1820) bring us into touch with almost every economic activity characteristic of the eighteenth century. We are introduced to the French economists devoted to Agriculture, the demographers like Süssmilch absorbed in vital statistics, the rising English political economy, with Cantillon, Adam Smith, Steuart, James Anderson, and Malthus as its prophets. Arthur Young and Malthus, late in the period, exchanged letters on Population and agriculture.[1]

Yet in respect of theories Young was not wholly identified with any of the individuals or schools mentioned. He considered himself as entirely a practical man, and contributed nothing directly to the theory of Population.

Like political economy itself, the theory of Population is no mere announcement of formulas. It is the critical judgment passed upon various concurring (or conflicting) elements and tendencies. A formula like Dunning Macleod's *Credit is Capital* is simple at the expense of truth, which means it would at the best be a half-truth. Such were some of the propositions laid down by Malthus in his first *Essay* of 1798. Such would have been the famous saying of Arthur Young himself: "The magic of property turns sand to gold"—if he had himself taken it as more than a passing remark.

Among the elements entering into a theory of Population the material forces of production must find a place, whether for agricultural production or manufacturing, and account must be taken of both in general economic theory. Technically there had been many inventions, from the beginning of the eighteenth century, with little pause. Richard Cantillon, now usually regarded as the first to see such things steadily together and view them as a whole, included both agriculture and manufacture in his *Essai sur le Commerce en général*, 1755. The title (say "Essay on Trade in general") does not cover the whole, but the writer does so, considering not merely the exchange of products, but the machinery of production preceding it, as a general problem for all cases where trade occurs at all. His book had great influence on the French economists, with whom Agriculture held the chief place. In Adam Smith's *Wealth of Nations*, 1776, it is rather Manufacturing Industry that is in the forefront, though, as in Cantillon's book, all the other elements are present and presented, including Population. But the "classical theory" of Population, Rent, and Value was only in germ a phenomenon of the eighteenth century. The mature form of it belongs to the early nineteenth.

Malthus, in the preface to the second edition of his *Essay*, puts Arthur Young among those who prepared the ground for his theory of Population. That author would receive the compliment with mixed feelings, professing to hate theories. In the Secretaryship of the Board of Agriculture,[2] with its voluminous published investigations, providing theorists with facts and figures, he ministered to the theory of Rent, in an indirect manner; and his utterances on Population are, for the most part and when he is off his guard, couched in the language of the later "classical school". But he had no intention of making contributions to economic, or indeed any other kind of, theory. As a practical man who did his work to admiration he served theory better than if he had set up as a theorist. We shall find theorists like Malthus writing to him, in order to draw upon his experience. The theorists exist to help the practical men, the practical men to help the theorists.

Our Arthur Young[3] was the son of Arthur Young, of Bradfield Hall, Suffolk. The father was an Army chaplain, who wrote on *Idolatrous Corruptions in Religion*, 1734, and served with the Army in Flanders 1742, leaving a journal of travels to edify his son afterwards. The son refused Church, Army, and business. He had "a natural propensity for writing books", and wrote a political tract at seventeen. His mother passed over to him a small farm in her property, and his career was settled; he became a propagandist of scientific agriculture, preparing himself by four years' work on the farm, 1763 ff. Walter Harte, author not only of *Gustavus Adolphus* but of *Essays on Husbandry*, 1765, taught him the best way to put his views on paper. He had speedy success; much more of it than on his own farm.

Miss Betham Edwards, in her preface to his *Autobiography*, says truly: "Whether regarded as the untiring experimentalist and dreamer of economic dreams, as the brilliant man of society and the world, or as the blind, solitary victim of religious melancholia, the figure before us remains unique and impressive." To the general reader he is known even now by his *Travels in France*, printed in 1792— a record of journeys made in 1787 to 1790 with the same purpose as his many English journeys, but happily including Paris at the Revolution.

Sir John Sinclair, who was not always in his "good books", certainly pleased him once by telling him that he (Arthur Young) had saved a man's life in the Revolution. Baron Silvestre "was in prison and brought to trial and told that his life should be saved if he could show that he had ever done anything useful to the Republic". When he told the Court that he had translated an abridgement of Arthur Young's *Travels in France* he was set at liberty.

The success of the early *Travels and Journeys*, beginning with the *Farmer's Letters* in two volumes, 1767, was, as he says himself in his *Autobiography*, largely due to his departure from convention. He was to the ordinary travellers over England as Charles Booth was to Mayhew in "description" of London. Instead of picturesque details of great mansions and their surroundings we have an account of soil, crop, stock, wages, and price. Not that he is insensible to the beauties of pictures and statues,[4] but, as he says in so many words, he judges a nobleman's greatness rather by the number of labourers on his land than by the number of footmen behind his chair. He was a born reporter, and the *Morning Post* engaged him to report the debates for them.[5] He says that, in his time, as things were in England, he could do no greater public service than stir men up to improve cultivation and thereby increase the supply of food, and to this faith at least he was constant through life. On the death of the Earl of Orford (1772) he wrote in his praise: "I leave the lieutenancy of a county, the rangership of a park, and the honours of the Bedchamber to those in whose eyes such baubles are respectable. I would rather dwell on the merit of the first importer of Southdown sheep into Norfolk." He criticized the King's bull and the King's hogs, but his relations with Farmer George were excellent.

He prided himself on being an experimentalist and having no general principles. As late as 1793 he writes: "I have been too long a farmer to be governed by anything but events."[6] "I have a constitutional abhorrence of theory." This would be pragmatism run wild, but he either does not really mean it, or he conveniently forgets it. We have appeals to principles and even to political economy. "I have through these papers laid it down as a principle that population is proportioned to employment"; and in the first of his books he writes: "Agriculture is the first and most important of all business[es] and the foundation which supports manufactures."

224

He is a link, though hardly a strong link, with the vital statisticians when he brings up the question of Depopulation, and takes stand against Price.[7] He helps our transition to Political Economy by his stand against the French Economists, with whom we might have supposed him naturally associated. So far as he was ever systematic he was so in the *Political Arithmetic containing Observations on the present State of Great Britain and the principles of her policy in the encouragement of Agriculture*, addressed to the "Oeconomical Societies established in Europe" (1774). It was really in part not only political arithmetic in the manner of Petty, but an endeavour after political economy in the manner of Cantillon and Hume. The preface begins: "The great encouragement which agriculture at present meets with in Europe has been either the cause or effect (probably both) of many publications upon that part of political economy which concerns the culture of the earth." These publications, he said, laid down principles contrary to his own both in legislation and business; and they showed great ignorance of what England had been doing. He thinks he can refute them from facts and "first principles".

So we have from him a good conspectus first of England's general conditions, in population, prices of food, luxury, land tenure, sizes of farms, enclosures, taxes, rates, and rents. He thinks England far from perfect in such matters, but it has avoided some French mistakes. The land tax of England falls on the landlord, and is not levied, like the French *taille*,[8] on the produce, to the discouragement of improvements. Rates certainly fall on the tenant, but he has allowed for them beforehand in the rent, which, with his eyes open, he agreed to pay. Tithes, he admits, are deterrent to improvements, but there are recognized compromises and adjustments. Lease should be universal. On Corn Laws he gives an uncertain sound because (he says) that is just what *they* do. He would keep the Bounty to prevent corn being too cheap as it was from 1730 to 1756. Cheapness is the ruin of industry, "no manufactures can flourish under it". He means cheap food, and pleads strongly for a high standard of living, quoting Houghton on Husbandry with approval. "It was good to encourage the people to a high living"[10]—a very bold idea but a very just one, he says. He might have found it also in Hume. It is the idea made familiar to us by Malthus. The opposite notion (he says) is involved in the return some writers advocate to the plain living of early Roman times. In order that we may have a greater population we are advised by some to parcel the land out into lots, each giving bare subsistence to a family. "Of what use in a modern kingdom would be a whole province thus divided, however well cultivated, except for the mere purpose of breeding men, which singly taken is a most useless purpose?" Such men would not give a market for any goods except their own; agriculture as a mere Means of Subsistence would not benefit the State; taken as a trade it does so greatly. And it is greatly helped forward by rising prices. Some will say that prices depend on quantity of money. He meets them by the distinction (though he does not use the words) of long and short periods, and depends on Hume's *Essays* for his views of the matter.[11]

The flourishing of agriculture, he says, is due to general wealth; from increase not of mere numbers but of luxury the farmer's market has increased. The people are living better, they have better food and more of it, and "drink a prodigiously greater quantity of beer", which, like Cobbett, he prefers to tea. One symptom too is the waste that goes on. Poverty would strike off all waste. The prime paradox of stock-raising is so stated: "In order to make beef cheaper you must make it dearer."[12] He was fond of paradoxes (using the very word), perhaps the best known being that high rents[13] are better for agriculture than low; and in the scarcity of 1804 he observes "the price must be really too high for the poor without being half high enough for the farmer". Toynbee quotes from the *Northern Tour*: To stop neglect in Cleveland, where thorns and briers were tolerated, "Raise their rents! First with moderation, and if that does not bring forth industry, double them." The paradox of the stock-raising is familiar enough to us in manufactured articles; he was probably the first to propound it of cattle. The case happens from time to time now, we are told, with hogs in the United States.

Apply similar reasoning to Population if we can.[14]

He tells us "Increasing the demand for a manufacture does not raise the price of labour; it increases the number of labourers in manufacture as a greater *quantum* or regularity of employment gives that additional value to the supply which creates the new hands." The demand gives that easy subsistence which plenty of land secures in America. Hence Birmingham increases because children are no burden, being employed as soon as they are old enough for employment. So will it be with agriculture (always his chief care). Emigrations actually add to the value of what remains, and so tempt to increase. How can you encourage reproduction more powerfully than by adding to the value of what is produced? "Labour is dearer in Holland than in any part of Europe; and therefore it is the most prosperous country in Europe." Franklin supports him, he says, in making Employment the main cause of population. The emphasis should be laid, not on plenty of food, but on plenty of employment, and that is just where engrossing and large farming, enclosing against the open field system, help us. Wallace[15] would have all manufactures laid aside for agriculture. But we need the larger market, the markets of manufactures, in order to make the best of our agriculture. In a later page Young says: "The farmer ought not to be tied down to bad husbandry, whatever may become of the population." Population is only a secondary object. A critic might urge that a complete theory should include the secondary objects, and also that the author was now making agriculture and its perfection an end in itself, as if it were obviously a better end in itself than population. But he is aware of the distinction between a population of poor quality and of high quality, and might have answered that his agriculture of high quality led to a population of high quality. What he does insist upon is the necessity of choosing that culture which is the more profitable. "The soil ought to be applied to that use in which it will pay most, without any idea of population"; hence he prefers enclosures.[16] If it be said that this is the language of a hard-hearted classical economist, the answer is that he is not more hard-hearted than Hume in the matter.

We were later to hear from him in the *Travels in France* that the French peasants effected marvels with poor soil "because, I suppose, their own". "The magic of property turns sand to gold."[17]

Young, as Mill[18] faithfully reminds us, was not a supporter of small properties as a rule, and is in fear of French subdivision. He does not desire for our people the excessive labour which the magic of property brings on the French peasant. "What an apparent contradiction (says Young) that property should be the parent of poverty; yet there is not a clearer or better ascertained fact in the range of modern politics." "The only property fit for a poor family is their cottage garden, and perhaps grassland enough to yield milk; this needs not of necessity impede their daily labour; if they have more they are to be classed with farmers, and will have arable fields which must in the nature of things be ill-cultivated, and the national interest consequently suffer." In other words, the labourer, becoming a farmer, would be running a business, with all the risks and difficulties of business, without the requisite training for business.

Hume, touching on the same problem, anticipates a modern incident of our own century: "'Tis a violent method, and in most cases impracticable to raise from the land more than what subsists [a man] himself and family. Furnish him with manufactures and commodities and he will do it of himself. Afterwards you will find it easy to seize some part of his superfluous labour and employ it in the public service without giving him his wonted return." This is the Exchequer's view of the matter rather than the cultivator's; but the idea is that it may lead to the benefit of the cultivator at the expense of his immediate pleasure.

Arthur Young was right in appealing to Hume, for this is how Hume proceeds in the same chapter: "It may seem an odd position that the poverty of the common people in France, Italy, and Spain is in some measure owing to the superior riches of the soil and happiness of the climate; and yet there want not many reasons to justify this paradox." One man "with a couple of sorry horses" will cultivate in a season "as much land as will pay a pretty considerable rent to the proprietor." All the art the farmer knows is to leave exhausted ground fallow for a year. The poor peasants need only a simple maintenance: they have no stock nor riches which claim more, "no stock but their own limbs, and they are entirely dependent on their landlord. In England the land "must be cultivated at great expense, and produces slender crops when not carefully managed, and by a method which gives not the full profit, but in a course of several years. A farmer therefore in England must have a considerable stock and a long lease, which beget proportional profits. Necessity is the great spur to industry and invention."

This passage of Hume may be turned into a commentary on the passage of Arthur Young on the hard work of the smallholders. France is still, in the twentieth century, a land of smallholders, the most industrious and parsimonious in the world. If Arthur Young could see them now he would repeat that, if we are to be as they are, for they are prosperous above others, we must work as they do, which we have never yet done in England.[19]

These views on Population prepare us for Arthur Young's decided stand against Richard Price. Employment not having been greater in earlier times, population could not have been so. If employment has increased, the people must have increased with it.[20] This argument is worked out elaborately against Price. Young quotes the elder Mirabeau as saying, "Consumption is the mother of production", and Quesnay on "Grains", in addition to Graunt and Petty. He acknowledges that the Poor

Law especially, because of the law of settlement, has been an obstacle, and that Norfolk has declined where it ought on his principles to have fared no worse than other places. Perhaps his happiest hit is that a great early population cannot be inferred from the extraordinary number of churches in Norfolk, for the pious founder[21] had no other way of perpetuating his memory than by churches: "A great man's memory may outlive his life half a year; but by 'r lady he must build churches then"—whether wanted or not. He sums up his case against Price neatly in the letter to *St. James's Chronicle*.[22]

But, if Young writes in a more lively style, John Howlett has put the case with more convincing completeness in his *Examination of Dr. Price's Essay*, 1781, where he does not fail to compliment Arthur Young and quotes nearly two pages from him.[23] Young's best service to the settlement of the question lay in his constant pleading for a Census, the need of which was felt by all investigators. Under the date 1771 he says: "I published my *Proposals for numbering the People*, the occasion of which was the Earl of Chatham's words: 'When I compare the number of our people estimated highly at seven millions, with the population of France and Spain usually computed at 25 millions, I see a clear self-evident possibility for this country to contend with the united powers of the House of Bourbon, merely upon the strength of its own resources.' I conceived that to draw such political principles for the national conduct from a mere supposition of population was a doctrine tending to very mischievous errors. I therefore was convinced that an actual enumeration of the people ought to take place."[24]

He would not himself have counted this *Proposal* his highest flight. He seems prouder to have been the introducer of chicory into England; to have done that was not to have lived in vain. His favourite among his books was that on Wastes, *Inquiry into the Propriety of applying Wastes to the better Maintenance of the Poor.* This is not the *Observations on the Present State of the Wastelands in this Kingdom*, 1772. The *Inquiry* appeared thirty years afterwards, namely, in 1801, and is discussed by Malthus in his *Essay* at the end of a long criticism of Arthur Young's schemes of reform.

"The Plough",[25] as he said, was always before him; it is much better to make experiments than to write books. So at Milan, October 6, 1789: "This day has passed after my own heart, a long morning, active, and then dinner, without one word of conversation but on agriculture." "If they [the Abbeys] contained the register of their ploughs, they would have been interesting; but what to me are the records of gifts to convents, for saving souls that wanted probably too much cleaning for all the scrubbing-brushes of the monks to brighten!" He could enjoy Leonardo and Cimarosa and admired Lawrence Sterne. But his heart was in Agriculture.

All the more are we surprised to find him out of sympathy with the French Economists. Of the Margrave of Baden[26] he writes: "The œconomistes [sic] speak much of an experiment he made in their Physiocratical rubbish, which [experiment], however erroneous their principles might be, marked much merit in the prince."

What, then, does he think wrong in them? He does not go back to Cantillon, but rather to their other origins, taking them as they looked to him in 1774. He does not seem to have read Cantillon. In the *Political Arithmetic* he gives a list embracing Quesnay, Mirabeau, Du Pont, Mably, Baudeau, and St. Peravy, but not Cantillon.

As "all for agriculture" was the motto of both Arthur Young and the French Economists, the somewhat bitter censure may illustrate the saying that a man's foes are those of his own household: "They are my brethren, hence this rage and sorrow." Both ask: "If so near, why not wholly on our side?" But Young did not come over, and he founded no rival sect which they might have exchanged for their own.

Young tells the others they got their argument from Locke and Decker, who suppose all taxes to be passed on except those levied on the landlord, who has no one on whom to shift his burden. You, he says, declare that this not only is but ought to be, for the land is the only producer.[27] What you would really do would be to "force a man to pay, not because he consumes but because he possesses".

Now his consumption of taxed articles really depends on himself, and therefore shows whether he is able to pay or not; to be forced to pay is no test of ability to pay. How would it answer in Holland, where there are many and heavy taxes, but no fertile lands to which they could all be transferred? The transference is supposed to make all articles cheaper and the landlord's rent would go farther. The single tax, however, is to fall not on the gross but on the net produce; this means (says Young) that the better producer a farmer is the more he pays, to his discouragement. The English plan of land tax is better; no more for good than for bad crops. Young admits (as we have seen already) that our tithes offend in this particular. So much the worse for them, he says, they are no part of our glory. Yet the Economists are not always wrong; they are, for example, sometimes conscious that dearness is better than cheapness, a precious article of his own creed. Perhaps (he thinks) they thought the method of collecting taxes so bad that they desired to reduce the collecting to a minimum.

Young rejects the French Economists, but has no general theory of his own to substitute for theirs.

With Malthus he enters into an interesting correspondence on the question "whether the agricultural capital which had so much increased the produce of the country during the last twenty years and raised the rent of land independently of any change in the value of the currency, has been furnished chiefly by tenants or [by] landlords".

Malthus puts the question in a letter of February 6, 1816, adding that he has been helped by Young's *Enquiry into the Rise of Prices in Europe*, 1815. A second letter, of May 26, 1816, expresses pleasure that the facts furnished by Young, in reply, confirm the view which Malthus takes, namely, that "much the greater part of the capital that has been employed in these improvements has been generated on the land, and been ocasioned in no inconsiderable degree by the high prices".

Their agreement on this subject may have comforted Arthur Young for his severe treatment in the *Essay* of Malthus, second edition, 1803, chap. X; "Of the errors in different plans which have been proposed, to improve the condition of the poor." The passage remained in the following editions, and the chief object of attack was our author's pamphlet, *The Question of Scarcity Plainly Stated*, 1800, which had recommended allotments of half an acre for every labourer that had three children.

But our programme will not carry us into such questions. Arthur Young and Malthus both bestride the limits of the centuries. It is a question, if such limits are of force to bind writers at all. Malthus made his start in the eighteenth, and his main work was done in the nineteenth century. Arthur Young was more truly of the eighteenth, and his natural force in the new century abated year by year.

He had really carried out his announced intention of being only a practical man. We need to be content with his example, for he comes near to refusing us his precept. There will always be found supporters of the old adage, "Example is better than precept", to whom it is more than a half-truth; but, if the two things correspond to practice and theory, the pioneers of Vital Statistics and Political Economy have triumphed by holding them closely together.

REFERENCES TO CHAPTER VIII

1. See *Malthus and His Work*, 216, 423. To dates there given add 1816, Br. Mus. The Museum has letters of Young and Malthus, 1816, 1818, 1829. See below (Ref. 29).

2. Secretary of the Board of Agriculture. See *Autobiography*, 216. Sir John Sinclair, who was doing valuable work for the Statistics of Scotland—see Malthus, *Essay*, 1803, p. 13—claimed to be the father of the Board; he at least moved for it in the House of Commons, May 1793, and became its first Chairman. But the Secretary seems to have had the lion's share of the work. See art. "Board of Agriculture" in *Palgrave's Dictionary*.

3. For the family history and our author's early life see the *Autobiography* edited by Miss Betham Edwards (Smith Elder), 1898, esp. pp. 4, 8 22, 24, 29, and 33. For the incident of life-saving see *Autobiography*, 464, 465, and for our author's explanation of his own success see ib., 54.

4. See, e.g., *Six Weeks' Tour*, 1767, *Autob.*, p. 44, 2nd ed., 1769, pp. 194–200, concerning Lord Pembroke's art treasures. Compare *Farmer's Letters*, I. 319.

5. Debates—*Autob.*, 63, cf. 229, 230.
Praise of Orford—ib., 206. The King's bull, 224.
The King's hogs—ib., 322–3. The King good-naturedly answered that they were a present from Hanover, and therefore (no doubt by the old adage) above criticism. Compare 190.

6. Against all general principles—*Example of France a Warning to Britain*, 1793. (See *Tables Turned*, 1926, p. 16.)
Not consistent here—*Political Arithmetic*, 1774, Preface, IX, and p. 86. *Farmer's Letters to the People of England*, 1767, 3rd ed., 1771, vol. I, p. 4.

7. *Political Arithmetic*, 1774, pp. 66, 320, 350, compare 289; on Wallace, ib., 291.

8. *Taille—Political Arithmetic*, 1774, pp. 183, 184; compare on tithe, p. 18, of free corn trade, 276 seqq., compare 32, 33 (the County).

9. Cheap food not approved, 32, 33—but not only food. See 198, where he says the statesman should try to make the prices of all commodities rise.

10. High Living—110, 111. He might have found something like this in Hume's *Essays*, quarto of 1753, p. 300.
Breeding men—a useless purpose, etc.—*Political Arithmetic*, 47 seqq.

RALEIGH TO ARTHUR YOUNG

11. Money—*Political Arithmetic*, 50; compare 53, 116, 120 (against Steuart).

12. Paradox of stock-raising—*Political Arithmetic*, 58; compare 131, 132. High prices beget their own reduction.

13. Paradox of Rents—*Political Arithmetic*, 275; compare *Autobiography*, 402 (as to 1804), *Northern Tour*, II. 80, 83.

14. Application to Population—*Political Arithmetic*, 61; compare 62–72.

15. Wallace, *Dissertation on the Numbers of Mankind*, 1753, p. 27. See Arthur Young, *Political Arithmetic*, 291; compare 80, 81, 123, 270.

16. Enclosures—*Political Arithmetic*, 123.

Hume, *History of England*, cited 155 to 157 (with note), and the writer said to be one "whose political ideas have an acumen that distinguishes him in an uncommon manner" (155).

Arnold Toynbee, *Industrial Revolution* (ed. Rivington's), 1884, p. 89, admits that the changes going on in those times told in favour of scientific cultivation.

17. Magic of property—*Travels in France*, quarto of 1792, pp. 36, 37, 74.

18. Mill on Young—J. S. Mill, *Political Economy*, II. VI. 7; Peasant Proprietors, p. 280 of Ashley's ed., 1909. Compare Young, *Travels in France*, 407, 410; cf. 391. Hume, *Essays*, quarto 1758, p. 154 of essay I on Commerce. For Hume's paradox, 156, 157. Compare Böhm Bawerk, *Positive Theorie des Kapitales*, 3rd ed., Innsbruck, 1909, Book II, especially Sections I and II, pp. 143–172. One of Böhm's main points is that in most cases the long way is more productive than the short way of production. The "long way" corresponds to Hume's "method, which gives not the full profit, but in a course of several years".

19. The industriousness of the French people is sometimes veiled for us by the luxuriousness of Paris, for which foreigners are largely answerable. Gibbon's Alexandria (chapter X, section II, *Decline and Fall*) has some striking features in common.

20. *Political Arithmetic*, 61–84; cf. 59 and 85.

Mirabeau, *Philosophie Rurale*, 1763.

Quesnay on "Grains" quoted in *Political Arithmetic*, 74. *Éphémérides du Citoyen*, ib., 202, 252. Petty, ib., 88, 153.

21. Pious founder, *Political Arithmetic*, 99.

22. *St. James's Chronicle* of March 28, 1752. *Political Arithmetic*, 322–331 (Appendix IV).

23. Howlett, pp. 32–34 from *Political Arithmetic*, 149, 150. Compare Young's *Autobiography*, 97.

24. Proposals for numbering the people. The full title is: "Pro-

posals to the Legislature for numbering the people, containing some observations on the Population of Great Britain, and a sketch of the advantages that would probably accrue from an exact knowledge of its present State. Dated 1772."

As to the date, the diary was not written from day to day. See *Autobiography*, 57, 58, and compare *Political Arithmetic*, 1774, p. 269 n., which gives the presumably right date, 1772.

Other titles to fame: chicory, *Travels in France*, 113; Wastes, Inquiry of 1801. Compare Malthus, *Essay*, 1803, IV. X. 580 n.; Young, *Autobiography*, 59, 350.

25. The plough—*Travels*, ib., 208; compare 153, Milan 201, cf. 204, 257.

26. Marquis of Baden—*Travels*, ib., 141. See Henry Higgs, *Physiocrats*, pp. 84, 86, where we read that Mirabeau's convert, the Marquis of Baden, tried the experiment in three of his villages.

Young gives a list of the Physiocrats from Quesnay, Mirabeau, etc., *Political Arithmetic*, 209 seqq., 1774.

We might apply to Young what Gibbon says of the Neoplatonists (*Decline and Fall*, chap. XIII, p. 52, of vol. II, ed. 1823): "As they agreed with the Christians in a few mysterious points of faith, they attacked the remainder of their theological system with all the fury of civil war."

28. Tithes, *Political Arithmetic*, 190 seqq.; compare 224, 227, 236. He does not mention *L'Homme aux Quarante Écus*, Voltaire, 1768.

He speaks of Steuart's refutation of the Economists—probably referring to *Political Economy*, Book V, chapters IX–XI. Compare Preface, XII, and Book I, XX, 188 of vol. I or *Works*, ed. by Steuart's son, 1805.

29. See British Museum: Arthur Young's correspondence purchased in 1897. Add. MSS. 35126 to 35133. The letters are in vol. VIII, 1815–1820, 35133. For other references of Malthus to Young see 2nd *Essay*, 1803, p. IV; *Political Economy*, 2nd ed., 1836, Book II chap. I, § 3, especially 286, 287. Compare *Malthus and His Work* (Unwin), 2nd ed., 423.

RETROSPECT

RETROSPECT

We began with definitions and descriptions of demography, vital statistics, theory of population.

We then tried, by glancing over a series of selected leaders, of thought, mainly in England, and mainly within the bounds of the two centuries, seventeenth and eighteenth, to discover what views on those subjects are to be gathered from those men. We found, a step farther back, Botero in Italy with clearer views on population than our own countrymen, among whom there are only at first loosely connected or quite disconnected hints. As attention became more settled on our subjects, we had an exploration of lines of investigation, followed by broad general theories of the movement of population and the springs of it.

We began with Raleigh, in an atmosphere of Plantations, Plagues, and Wars. We learned from him to regard the Race, but not to forget the individual.

We were then taught by Bacon that the safety of a kingdom lies in a strong yeomanry; and we reminded ourselves that in his days defence would naturally seem more important than opulence. We consoled ourselves for his sermons on politics by his lessons on science in general. We could not pass over Hobbes, for, like David Hume, he inspired everyone else to write against him, including James Harrington, who speaks more to our purpose. "If you do not obey your ruling power", says Hobbes, "you will fall back into the old anarchy." "Quite so," says Harrington, "but how establish this same ruling power on the best and surest foundations? Let me answer: Power depends on property; and self-government is best secured where the amount of property held by individuals is limited and the citizens do not all hang by the teeth on a privileged few who feed them. In England, therefore, we must limit the income from land. It is true that in our Cities in 1656 there is another kind of property, sucking the breasts of the first, as actually Holland, the whole nation, sucks the breasts of the whole world, and depends on trade, commerce, manufacture." Harrington does not think of asking how it was that the Plague, the "bogey" or ugly features of the seventeenth century, did not wipe out his great cities; they sprang up again as soon as it had gone. By what miracle?

We observed that *Demography begins in these great cities* and not in the country districts; and John Graunt, the city magnate, with "his excellent working head", fastens on the London Bills of Mortality, brings out their meaning by setting them in order, and expounds the same in his memorable *Observations*. He is able to point to a power of population, both within and without the walls, that explains how the Plague was baffled. Then for the first time it was noticed that some secrets come out of large numbers which escape notice in small. This is a ruling principle of what we call Statistics. The larger numbers (let us say) are a magnifying-glass which discovers the secrets that the small numbers hold tight. The confused sounds of a railway train go together into a harmonious hum over the whole valley, at proper distance. There are many such analogies.

The growth of a generation of living beings (where there are casualties every day of the year and yet the whole goes marching on) is found to be a growth by law, rule, and measure, even allowing, as in other sciences, of a degree of prediction and calculation.

But we seem to hear Graunt saying, inarticulately enough: "You have given me too few facts, too few figures, or I could have done more for you. No census, no rural figures, baptisms instead of births, no marriages, no ages at death, frail old lady-Dogberries as 'searchers' instead of active young curates as registrars of deaths. Petty helped me to the figures of one country district, but what are these amongst so many?"

A score of years after Graunt, and when Petty too has gone, Halley presents better figures, from Breslau; he makes out of them the first full-formed *Life Table;* and, being himself of Pascal's rank, can so use Pascal's doctrine of Chances that he can estimate the probable further living of men or women of a given age. He can then place the price of Life Annuities and all ordinary Life Insurance on a rational basis, adapted for England. De Witt and Hodde had already done it for Holland, though the fates were against them in their own country in 1672.

From Halley's *Table* come Addison's Visions of Mirzah, of the Bridge of Human Life; and we saw the scientific reconstruction of the Bridge in Professor Karl Pearson's remarkable picture of *Death the Marksman.*

After Halley for some years we hear of spade-workers, great and small. Kersseboom, the father of Dutch demography, and Wargentin of Swedish, last and not least Johann Peter Süssmilch himself, the father of German demography, are men who devote their lives to the work, and are no casual spade-workers. If Derham really brought Süssmilch to the knowledge of Graunt he did well; and Derham's book shows at least how the ideas of Graunt have become part and parcel of demography. "How glorious!" says Derham. Graunt's achievement is described by him and by Süssmilch as if it had been an English version of the famous and familiar Dutch reclamation of land from the barren sea. It was the saving for law and order of a whole new continent, with Graunt for the Columbus who discovers it.

Süssmilch, like Graunt, sighed for better data; but, as it is, he rejoices, with old Chief Justice Hale, that the numbers of the people go on increasing, and increasing in a now intelligible manner.

Süssmilch makes the most of everything he gets, whether on the Continent or in England. To him

Hume is a better guide than Montesquieu; Hume is right in thinking that the Ancients had not a greater but a smaller population than ours. This is his link with Hume, who is more economist than demographer.

It is time for the economists to take over the whole theory of Population and study it in its relation to their general economic theory, just beginning to grow up. They have no need to care about the antiquarian disputes concerning ancient Learning and ancient Populousness; but at this point there is a doubt raised that interests them, about the Populousness of our own country since the Conquest, Richard Price, for example, maintaining a decline of it. That discussion becomes a stepping-stone to higher things. Robert Wallace, who in 1753 opposed Hume over the Ancients, proceeds eight years afterwards with greater zest to write another book, the *Prospects*, in which he looks as far *forwards* as before he has looked *backwards*; and he puts a shrewd question: "If the ideal State (of my *Prospects*) should come into being, would not our numbers grow too fast—would this little globe hold us all? We are not too many now simply because of our iniquities; is it not clear that we are never meant to be free from our iniquities and reach the Ideal? Are we doomed to sin, for ever, that we may live on this planet at all?

Richard Price does not pay much attention to the visions of Wallace, having visions of his own. He may be called reactionary in his attitude to the question of England's population. But he stimulates other men to think on subjects where his own thinking is far from profound; and in the matter of theory we are largely indebted to him for Burke's political philosophy and for the Malthusian theory of population. Malthus confesses also his obligations to the practical men like Arthur Young, but it was a debt very different both in kind and in degree.

Professor Karl Pearson kindly took the chair when the lectures were delivered. The last two chapters of this book were never delivered as lectures, and it seemed the frankest course to convert the whole into chapters of a book. The book has no pretensions to be anything more than an introduction to a study of the subjects. Its example may turn out to be a better service than its precepts; and, if the present writer could foresee the coming of a more learned treatise to perfect these beginnings, the pleasure of that hope would be his great reward.

INDEX

INDEX

INDEX

INDEX